NICHOLAS BERDYAEV

The Crisis of Art

(1918)

(Klepinina № 14)

Translated by Fr. S. Janos

frsj Publications

The Crisis of Art

Copyright © 2018 by translator Fr. Stephen Janos

ISBN: 978-0-9963992-9-6 *Hardcover*
ISBN: 978-0-9991979-0-5 *Paperback*

Library of Congress Control Number: 2018907250

No part of this book may be reproduced or transmitted in any form or by any means, graphic, electronic, or mechanical, including photocopying, recording, taping, or by any information storage retrieval system, without the written permission of the copyright holder.

In the event of the eventual demise of the present copyright holder, in accord with United States copyright law, copyright of this work devolves to Andrew M. Janos, son/heir of Fr. Stephen Janos.

Printed in the United States of America

Printed on acid-free paper.

For information address:

frsj Publications
Fr. Stephen J. Janos
P.O. Box 210
Mohrsville, PA 19541

The Crisis of Art

Foreword to the English Edition i

The Crisis of Art 1
Picasso 21
An Astral Novel (A. Bely's "Peterburg") 27

Addenda

The Ivanov Wednesdays 39
Deadening Tradition 45
The Charm of the Affectations of Culture 53

The Russian Temptation (A. Bely's "Silver Dove") 65
Murky Visages (Andrei Bely / Aleksandr Blok) 81
The Liege-Knight of Poverty (Léon Bloy) 91

* * *

Threefold Triadic Hierarchy of Angelic Ranks 131

Foreword to the English Edition

N. A. Berdyaev's "The Crisis of Art", a booklet of 47 pages, appeared in 1918, a century ago. Well, better a century for the English translation to appear in print, than not at all. The 1918 booklet was comprised of 3 articles, the initial three articles of the present text, which has been expanded to nine correlated articles by Berdyaev from this period, suggestive of a threefold triadic schema, such as obtains with the angelic ranks (vide our ecclesial-sourced translation in concluding the present book, in clarification of this point).

Both the "Picasso" and the "Peterburg" articles provide a key intuition that threads together the initial Russian booklet, as well as the present expanded English text. In the "Picasso" visually, and in the "Peterburg" consciously everything has become disjointed, disconnected, disintegrated and dismembered within our perceptive association, from our comfortable everyday ordinary aspect. Everything has been thrown into uncertainty, nothing remains ascertained and sure. Why is this pertinent? Consider early 1918 in Russia, merely a few short months into the "Oktyabr Revolution" of 1917, when Lenin's Bolsheviks were just beginning to consolidate their grip and control over Russian life, when the uncertainty of a "tomorrow" for many became increasingly uncertain... When man lives uncertain of a "tomorrow", of any future, man lives in a state of heightened tension, at the "edge", the "existential moment" at the extreme. What is the "real" at such moments, when all the old assuredness of life goes hollow and crumbles before our eyes... Everything becomes subject to doubt, to uncertainty, as one attempts to ascertain what is authentically true and real and of value, rather than clichéd delusions... A man with ultimately no "tomorrow" is already a man of the Absolute, as our final Léon Bloy article suggests...

The second triad of articles concern Vyacheslav Ivanov, whom the initial "Crisis of Art" article mentions with the lost connection of theurgy within art. The basis of every artistic "culture" derives originally from the "cultus", the "religious cult" from which it springs forth. And when later on it loses its inward theurgic religious dynamic of participatory communion, its vigour fades, until finally it is fit only as a museum piece, for detached observers to find bemused entertainment with, and wherein a culture passes

Nicholas Berdyaev

over into a civilisation, bereft of soul... Sophisticated attempts at revival of a culture typically fail, since they produce mere "affectations of culture", as with Vyach. Ivanov, along with the detachedly "objective" scholarly community generally... whom as Christ once noted, "In seeing they see not, and in hearing they fail to understand" (Mk. 4:12)...

In the final triad of Berdyaev articles in our text, the two A. Bely related articles represent chronological outliers. The "Russian Temptation" was written the earliest, in 1910, and the "Murky Visages" was written latest, in 1923, with Berdyaev already banished from Russia. The former article, on Andrei Bely's 1910 novel, "The Silver Dove", in rather sexual a metaphor represents a critique of the Russian Intelligentsia's worship of the Russian people, the "narod", a conjugal failure, indeed prophetic in its final tragic results. The "Murky Visages" article refers both to A. Bely, and to his reminiscences of the Russian poet, Aleksandr Blok, who had died shortly before, in 1921. In both the aesthetic and also the academic scholarly soul, often there obtains a failure in "the discerning of spirits", where evil appears under the guise of the good. In A. Blok's surreal poem, "The Twelve", Christ is depicted as leading the bloody carnage of revolution (as has "liberation theology" horrendously). The murky aspect of Russian sophiology, deriving from Vl. Solov'ev, likewise has proved so romantically charming to religiously ungrounded academics...

The driving impetus, indeed urgency, to the present book appearing now, is this -- the by-chance providential discovery of Berdyaev's 1914 article entitled "Рыцарь нищеты (Léon Bloy)". Already years back the other articles of our text had been translated, pen on paper, with the ink now threatening to fade... But the L. Bloy article remained just another intriguing title, nowhere to be found. One tended to imagine that it concerned some French revolutionary champion of social justice, like so many another...

And then, a few short months back, like an angelic heralding came the hint from L. H., that it could be found on the Internet, and after arduous a search it indeed was found at but one site. What a jewel, what a treasure! It had been incorporated into a year 2005 Russian translation of three of L. Bloy's booklets and entitled, "Кровь бедняка" (izdanie by Russkii Put', Moskva, 284 pages). The press run of 2000 copies quickly vanished into the vastness of Russia, the news never making it across to our far-Western shores... And it should be noted, *very importantly indeed, that the unique significance of Berdyaev's 1914 article on Léon Bloy, with its lengthy*

THE CRISIS OF ART

extracts in Russian translation and also lengthy French excerpts, was precisely in this,-- that for nearly a century, ninety years, Berdyaev's article was the only "Russian source" on Léon Bloy, until the year 2005.

Initially, before becoming immersed in translating the text, was the matter of the title, which simply translated, is "The Knight of Poverty", somewhat too bland. In our uncouth modern day, the image of the valiant knight, a man of noble valour and bearing, has lost its lustre, has grown rusty in our cynical age. Initially, to provide proper a nuance, the translator toyed with the archaic term "Paladin", an echo from the heroic "La Chanson de Roland" epic, but L. Bloy proves not to be of this noble visage. Finally seemed appropriate "Liege-Knight", aa s medieval fighter honour bound in fealty to his "liege-lord". And similarly the translator has indulged in a certain degree of license, rendering "Le Mendiant ingrat" as "Indigent Ingrate" rather than "Ungrateful Beggar", since many a beggar tends not to be overly grateful... Artistic linguistic whims of a translator...

Léon Bloy is credited with bringing from atheism to the Catholic faith the later illustrious Thomist Scholastic thinker, Jacques Maritain and his wife Raisa (of Russian Jewish ancestry). Both L. Bloy and the Raisa Maritain connection help explain the strong bond of friendship that later developed between J. Maritain and Berdyaev, despite the disparities of their philosophic approach.

Who was Léon Bloy? Berdyaev's article opens a window into a current of French literature totally new, totally unknown, for both the translator and perchance most readers. At first sight, at first impression, one is repelled, extremely so, by his vile mannerisms, by his nasty crude turns of expression, viciously uncouth, unsettling. He is a man obsessed, a totally impossible and irascible fellow, the sort one typically goes out of the way to avoid. He is a man obsessed with the Absolute, in context of the "existential now", a man without a tomorrow or the day after. L. Bloy was roughly contemporaneous with Friedrich Nietzsche, and in photos of both there is the same look of near-madness in the eyes. And there are other affinities to both. But whereas Nietzsche retreated to a mountainous lofty abode of isolation, L. Bloy descended into the lowlands muck of life. And if memory serves correctly, Nietzsche in his descent into madness identified with "Christ Crucified", as did L. Bloy sensing himself as co-crucified with Christ, obsessively as it were refusing to let Christ be taken down from the Cross, in its final significance of the Resurrection...

Nicholas Berdyaev

Léon Bloy is the "by-birth by-blood" sort of Catholic, as likewise also the sort of Protestant, and of Orthodox, and even atheist, that one too often chances to meet. Yet with L. Bloy there is something far more than with this droll sort. One is initially repelled, turned off by this irascible and loathesome fellow. As Berdyaev states, L. Bloy belongs to no current, and no current would be comfortable having him. And yet, after the initial disagreeable impression, one becomes nonetheless fascinated by him, "spellbound" by him. As Berdyaev tends to note, Léon Bloy in a sense follows in the tradition of Russia's "Holy Fools" ("юродиви"), who like L. Bloy provoked harsh and abusive reactions and mockery, provoking the blows and insults therein to glorify God in the image of the mockery of Christ upon the Cross -- "He saved others, yet Himself He cannot save..." (Mk. 15:31-32). And in the final end, one perceives that one has actually experienced the perspicacity of a seer. L. Bloy is obsessed with poverty, he gloats in it, and yet his embrace of poverty, which as a Christian he esteems more highly than love, is so dissimilar in spirit from how St. Francis of Assisi embraced it, joyfully, as Berdyaev notes.

How extraordinarily peculiar is Léon Bloy's image of both himself, and of God, as of "the hand of one raised against all, and against whom all hands are raised". So very like with a criminal on the lam, -- a dangerous insight that blindly can lead to the tragic results of Dostoevsky's Raskol'nikov and Kirillov. (And moreover strange, is it not, that while Berdyaev stresses L. Bloy's narrow-minded French horizon, Berdyaev teases us with the passing suggestion that Bloy has read such Russians as Dostoevsky and A. Herzen!). Bloy's radical perception of the "aloneness", not only of the individual man, but even moreso of the very God, is indeed striking. "Aloneness", the pervasive sense of "forsakenness", is far different a thing than mere "loneliness". We typically think of "aloneness" as moreso characteristic of the Devil ("alone, always ever alone"), than as regards God. And as Berdyaev cautions, there is in Bloy's thought and extremism a fine line of separation, nigh close to the demonic at times, requiring a "discerning of spirits". The "aloneness" of the individual person in his existential setting is indicative of course of the sense of "alienation" experienced in modern society and pseudo-community. But the "aloneness" as experienced by God, opens entirely new a dimension of thought. There is a most remarkable painting by the Russian artist, Ivan Kramskoy, entitled "Christ in the Wilderness", that in dramatic and vivid intensity captures this sense of the "aloneness" of God (we urge the reader to view

THE CRISIS OF ART

the image via the Internet). The absolutely arid landscape, the tightly gripped hands, stooped shoulders, taunt facial expression, a twilight of uncertain dawning or fading day -- all this dramatically conveys visually the point of L. Bloy's extraordinary intuition.

And finally, there is Léon Bloy's radical philosophic significance with his exposé of the "metaphysics of bourgeoisness". Something that only a Frenchman of acerbic wit and acid pen might effectively venture. For L. Bloy, the "bourgeois" is not some mere convenient socio-political label for self-smug intellectual activists to toss about, the "bourgeoisness" rather is a poisoned "bad-faith" characteristic at the very core of the human consciousness. Unlike Nietzsche, who recourses off upon the "high road", Bloy takes the "low road" into the thicket of the issue. In his own way, L. Bloy remains "joined at the hip" with the bourgeoisness that he so despises, in his obsession unable to free himself of its taint. It reminds one of Melville's Ahab, entangled upon the white whale, with the free hand beckoning us to come follow into the descent into madness. Berdyaev extensively quotes in French from L. Bloy's work, "The Explication of Commonplace Sayings", with brutally honest insights. The "metaphysics of bourgeoisness" opens the path towards much needed further profound philosophic insights.

Some insights of L. Bloy carry over into Berdyaev's own thought. One such is the intuition of the *unrepeatably unique individual human person, the significance of whose unrepeatable fate and destiny is known ultimately only to God*. His varied emphasis upon this theme is what renders Léon Bloy exceptionally a Christian existentialist, a Christian personalist philosophic figure, of notable a stature, in the opinion of this translator, far indeed exceeding suchlike personages as Kierkegaard et al. Léon Bloy indeed richly deserves further scrutiny.

Fr. S. Janos

18 June 2018

The Crisis of Art

The Crisis of Art

(1918 - #14,1)[1]

Art has survived many a crisis over its history. The transitions from antiquity to the Medieval and from the Medieval to the Renaissance betoken such profound crises. But that, which is occurring with art in our epoch, cannot be termed merely one crisis in a series of others. We are present at a crisis of art in general, amidst the deepest tremours within its thousand year old foundations. The old ideal of the classically beautiful art has become ultimately tarnished, and there is a feeling for a return to its images. Art has convulsively striven to go beyond its limits. The borderlines have shattered, such as distinguish one art from another and indeed art in general from that, what yet already is not art, from what is higher or lower than it. There has never yet been so acutely put the problem of the relation of art to life, of creativity and existence, never yet has there been such a thirst to pass over from the creativity of producing art to a creativity of life itself, new life. There is awareness of an impotence of the creative act of man, a lack of correspondence between the creative task and the creative realisation. Our time knows simultaneously both an unprecedented creative boldness and an unprecedented weakness. The man of the utmost final creative day wants to create something never before existing and in his creative rapture oversteps all the bounds and all the limits. But this finalistic man fails to create any yet so perfect and beautiful

---

[1] KRIZIS ISKUSSTVA. Published originally as the lead article to the Pamphlet (Kl. № 14) entitled as "Krizis Iskusstva, Sbornik statei" ("The Crisis of Art, a Collection of Articles"), Moscow, 1918, publisher G. A. Leman and S. I. Sakharov, 47 pages. Within this 3-article anthology, the second article is reprint from 1914 (Kl. № 174), -- "*Picasso*"; and the third article is reprint from 1916 (Kl. № 233), -- "*An Astral Novel: A. Bely's "Peterburg"*".

Berdyaev's "The Crisis of Art" article has subsequently been reprinted in tom 2 of the 1994 Liga Moscow Russian text, "Philosophia, tvorchestva, kul'tury i iskusstva", c. 399-418.

products, such as were created by the more unassuming man of former epochs.

From opposing ends there is to be noticed a crisis of the old art and the search for new paths. In modern art can be discerned strivings synthetic and strivings analytic, currents diametrically opposite. Both the strivings towards a synthesis of arts, towards their confluence into a single mystery, and the opposite strivings towards an analytic dissection within each art, tend simultaneously to shake the bounds of each art, and simultaneously also they signify a profound crisis of art. The synthetic strivings have been noted already with Mallarmé [Stéphane, 1842-1898]. And in a very vivid decorative setting there was the musical drama of R. Wagner. The Symbolists were the bearers of these synthetic strivings. Certain of them wanted to lead art out of the crisis through a return to the organic artistic era. The arts -- are a product of differentiation. They -- are derived from a temple and cultic origin, they developed from a certain organic unity, in which all the parts were subordinated to a religious centre. Many of the Symbolists of our generation and the generation before dreamt about restoring to art a significance both liturgical and sacral. The sacral art of the ancient world and of the Medieval world, the most vividly organic epochs within the history of human culture, remained for them enticing and captivating, and the call of the past for them was stronger than the call for the future. We are living out the end of the Renaissance, we are experiencing the final remnants of that epoch, when the human powers were set free and their bedazzling unfolding begat beauty. At present this free unfolding of human powers has passed over from regeneration into degeneration, it no longer still creates the beautiful. And there is an acute sense of the inevitability of a new direction for the creative powers of man. Man has become too much free, too much the release from his empty freedom, too much the exhaustion from the prolonged critical epoch. And man has come into an anguished yearning within his creativity for organicity, for a synthesis, for a religious centre, for mystery.

A very brilliant theoretician of these synthetic-organic strivings amongst us is Vyacheslov Ivanov [1866-1949]. To the Futurists he would seem very archaic. His preaching of sobornost'-communality in art is oriented backwards, to the ancient sources of art and culture. He -- is eternally the Alexandrian as regards his outlook, and like an Alexandrian, he experiences the sobornost', the organic and sacral aspect of the ancient and archaic Greece. When Vyach. Ivanov preaches a theurgic art, his

THE CRISIS OF ART

preachings then bear reminiscences and reflections of the old cultures. The theurgic idea is great. But a theurgic foundation for contemporary art could easily come to be transformed into a norm thrust on from the outside, a residue from the remote past. The sobornost' aspect with V. Ivanov is not at all something immanent for our times, rather instead is quite transcendent for it. V. Ivanov himself -- is a remarkable poet, but his theoretical strivings in our epoch, lacking in an awareness of sobornost', can prove dangerous for the autonomy of art. In the art of painting, Chiurlenis [Mikaloius Konstantinas, 1875-1911] has represented an expression of synthetic aspirations. He goes beyond the bounds of painting as a distinct and autonomous art and seeks to synthesis painting with music. He attempts within a musical painting to express his own cosmic feeling, his own clearly evident contemplation of the complexion and construct of the cosmos. He is both remarkable and interesting as regards his strivings. But the painting of Chiurlenis is inadequate to his visions, it is an incomplete transformation of them into a different language, as it were. He is picturesquely helpless, the painting insufficiently elaborated and the history of painting unenriched by new norms. The painting of Chiurlenis -- is a very characteristic example of what, as synthetic strivings, can have destructive effects upon art, and in any case, would express a profound deficiency for art: the striving towards a synthesis of the arts and the subjoining of mysticism to art can be destructive of the artistic form. Immeasurably more powerful is another expresser of synthetic strivings. I have in mind the revolutionary genius of Scriabin. In modern art I know of no one else, in whom there has been such a rapturous creative outburst, devastating the old world and laying the foundations for a new world. The musical genius of Scriabin is so great, that in music he has managed adequately to express his own new and catastrophic world-sense, to extract from the dark depths the existence of sounds, which the old music had ignored. He wanted to create a mysterium, in which would be synthesised all the entirety of art. And the mystery he conceived of eschatologically. It should have to be the end of this world. All the creative values of this worldly aeon, towards which we approach, would enter into the mystery. And this world would end, when there resound the sounds of this finalative mystery. The creative vision of Scriabin is unprecedented in its boldness, but scarcely is it likely that he will bring it to realisation. And yet he himself is an astonishing phenomenon of the creative path of man. This creative path of man makes art obsolete in the old and seemingly eternal sense of the word. The synthetic searchings give a pull towards mysterium and by this they go out beyond the bounds not only of the separate arts, but also of art in general. What however happens with art in its modern analytic aspirations?

The positings of a verymost profound crisis of art are not the result of the synthetic searchings, but of rather the analytic searchings. The searchings for a synthesis of art, the searchings after a mysterium, the attempts at a return to an art liturgical and sacral has as its representatives remarkable thinkers and creative people, but in them there is much preserved from the old and eternal art, and it is not ultimately shaken down to its foundations. In the strivings towards synthesis nothing is dissociated, the cosmic winds do not carry off the artist-creators and the artistic creations from those age-old spots, which are prepared for them within the organic structure of the earth. Even within the revolutionary art of Scriabin there is to be noted not so much a dissociation and dissolution, as rather the conquests of new spheres. But with Scriabin there was even too great a faith in art, and his bonds with the great past were not sundered. An altogether different nature and different sense obtains in those phenomena, which I term as the analytic aspirations in modern art, shattering and sundering every organic synthesis both of the old natural world and of the old art. Cubism and Futurism in all its manifold hues appears an expression of these analytic strivings, shattering all organicity. These waftings of a final day and final hour of human creativity ultimately disintegrate the old beautiful embodied art, always connected with antiquity, with the crystalising forms of the flesh of the world. The most remarkable results of this tendency obtain in painting.

A genius-endowed representative of Cubism is the artist Picasso. When one gazes upon a picture by Picasso, one then tends to think belaboured thoughts.[1] "The happiness of an embodied life under the sunlight has vanished. The wintry cosmic wind has stripped away the veil behind the veil, all the flowers and the leaves have become scorched, stripping away the skin of things, all that was clothed has fallen away, all

---

[1] I am citing here from certain places of the article about Picasso, which follows further on. For the construction of my "Crisis of Art" text, Picasso is necessary by way of example, and by which I develope my own thought about art. Paraphrasing myself however I consider bad form.

the flesh, manifest in images of incorruptible beauty, has dissipated. It comes to seem, that never will ensue the cosmic Springtime, never will there be the leaves, the greenery, the beautiful veilings, the embodied synthetic forms. It comes to seem, that after the terrible Winter of Picasso the world will not yet blossom forth, as before, that in this Winter will fall away not only all the veils, but likewise all the objective corporeal world will become unhinged down to its very foundations. There transpires as it were a mysterious coming apart of the cosmos. All more and more it becomes impossible to posit a synthetically-whole artistic apperception and creativity. Everything analytically is dissolved and dismembered. By means of such an analytic dismemberment the artist intends to get down to the very skeleton of things, down to the solid forms, hidden behind the softening veils. The material veilings of the world have begun to disintegrate and shred apart and there is the searching out of the solid substances, hidden behind this softening. In his searching out of the geometric forms of objects, the skeleton of things, Picasso has arrived at a stone age. But this -- is an illusory stone age. The gravity, the solidness and welding together of the geometric figures of Picasso only seems so. In actuality the geometric bodies of Picasso, assembled from the cubic skeletons of the corporeal world, fall apart from the slightest shake. The final layer of the material world, revealing itself to Picasso the artist after stripping away all the veils, -- is illusory, and not real. Picasso -- is a merciless exposer of the illusion of an embodied, materially synthetic beauty. Behind the captivating and alluring feminine beauty he sees the terror of disintegration, dissolution. He, in his sharp-sightedness, sees through all the veilings, the covering cloths, in layers there also, in the depths of the material world, he sees its own deposits of the monstrous. This -- is the demonic grimacings of the fettered spirits of nature. To go still further in depth, and for there still to be no sort of materiality, -- there already is the inward structure of nature, of the hierarchy of spirits. Painting, just like all the plastic arts, had been an embodiment, a materialisation. The highest upsurges of the old painting provided a crystalised and formalised flesh. Painting was connected with a firmness of the embodied physical world and stability of formal matter. But now at present painting is experiencing an as yet unprecedented crisis. If one penetrate the further into this crisis, then it becomes impossible to term it otherwise than as *a dematerialisation, a disembodied sort of painting.* In painting is transpiring something, it would seem, quite opposite the very nature of the plastic arts. Everything already as it were has become exhausted within the sphere of the embodied, materially-crystaline painting. In modern painting there is no spirit that becomes embodied, becomes materialised, and matter itself becomes dematerialised, becomes disembodied, and loses its solidity, its firmness and sense of form. Painting submerges itself into the depths of matter and there, in the very final layers, it finds there already no materiality. With Picasso the boundaries of physical bodies become unsteady. In modern art the spirit as it were tends to wane, and flesh to be dematerialised. This -- is a very deep jolting for the plastic arts, and which shakes the very essence of the plastic form. The dematerialisation in painting can produce the impression of the ultimate collapse of art. It would seem, that in nature itself, in its rhythm and cyclic-turns, that something irreversibly has fractured and changed. The world has altered its veilings. The material veilings of the world were merely temporary coverings. The age-old attire of being has rotted and fallen away".

All the firm delineations of being have shattered, become decrystalised, stretched apart, pulverised. Man passes over into the state of an object, objects pass over into the human state, one object passes over into another object, all the layers get jumbled, all the planes of being get confused. This new sense of world life attempts to find its expression in Futurist art. Cubism was but one of the expressions of this cosmic whirlwind, sweeping everything from its place. Futurism in all its manifold variations goes even further. This -- is a sequential shattering of the features of the settled state of being, the vanishing of all the definitely delineated images of the objective world. In the old, the seemingly eternal art, the image of man and the human body had firm contours, he was distinct from the images of other objects in the world, from minerals, plants and animals, from rooms, houses, streets and cities, from machines and from the infinitude of the worldly expanse. In Futurist art there are erased the boundaries, separating the image of man from other objects, from the enormous mechanical monstrosity, called the modern city. Marinetti proclaims in his manifesto: "Our bodies enter into the couches, upon which we sit, and the couches enter into us. The autobus is transformed into the houses, alongside which we drive past, and in their turn the houses rush at the autobus and pour off from it". The human image vanishes in this process of a cosmic stretching apart and pulverisation. The Futurists wanted as though with pathos to kill away and reduce to ashes the

THE CRISIS OF ART

image of man, always reinforced by the image of the material world separate from him. When the material world is sent reeling to its foundations, the image of man also is sent reeling. The world in its dematerialisation penetrates through into man, and man having lost his spiritual stability dissolves away in the diluted down material world. The Futurists demand a transferring of the centre of gravity from man over to matter. But this does not mean, that they can be called materialists in the old sense of the word. Man vanishes, as vanishes also the old matter, with which he corresponded. "To abolish the "I" within literature, i.e. to abolish all psychology" -- thus formulates Marinetti [Filippo, 1876-1944] one of the points of his programme. "Man does not represent any sort of absolutely greater an interest. And thus, expunge him from the literature. Chalk him up finally as matter, the essence of which it is necessary to grasp by bursts of intuition. Discern through his free objects and capricious motorings of breathing the sensation and instincts of metals, stones, trees, etc. Eliminate the psychology of man, henceforth empty, *with a lyrical impulse of matter*". "Of interest to us is the solidity of the steeliness of the plastic art per se, i.e. the non-conceptual and non-human union of its molecules and electrons, which resist, for example, the pull of the nucleus. The warmth of a bit of gland or of wood is more exciting for us, than the smile or the tears of a woman". "It is necessary, moreover, to catch the gravity and smell of objects, which up to now they have disdained to do in literature. To strive, for example, to convey the landscape of smells, perceptible by a dog. To hearken to motors and reproduce their utterances. Matter always has been investigated by an absent-minded and cold I, excessively concerned with itself, full of prejudicial wisdom and human impulses". The hostility to man, to the human "I" is clearly apparent in the Futurist manifesto of Marinetti. And herein lies concealed a fundamental contradiction of Futurism. The Futurists want to have the growth of an accelerated dynamic and yet they deny the wellspring of the creative dynamic -- man. There is no lever, by which the Futurism could flip over the world. There is no genuine dynamism within Futurism, the Futurists are situated in the grip of a certain worldwide whirlwind, not knowing the meaning of what is occurring with them, and essentially, remaining passive. They are obsessed with a certain sort of process, they spin round in it with an ever growing acceleration, but actively creative they are not. They are situated in the grip of a disintegration of the material world. Futurism possesses an enormous symptomatic significance, it indicates not only a crisis of art, but also a crisis of life itself. Regrettably, the agitational manifestos of the Futurists take precedence over artistic creativity. In these manifestos they express their own altered sense of life. But they are incapable to adequately express this new sense of life in the fashionings of art. This creative incapacity is especially to be sensed in the Futurist poetry and literature. What happens is a decrystalisation of words, a flattening down of words, sundering words apart from any sense of the Logos. But a new cosmic rhythm, a new sense of harmony the Futurists fail to detect. The problem with Futurism consists in this, that it is too oriented backwards, negatively attached to the past, too concerned with settling accounts with it and not at all with a passing over to a new creativity in freedom. It is merely a transitory state, moreso the end-point of the old art, rather than the construction of a new art. The Futurists perceive only on the surface the quite profound processes of change in human and world life. But they dwell in a verymost profound spirit of ignorance, with them there is no sort of spiritual knowledge of the meaning of what is occurring, not that intensive spiritual life, which would have made visible not only the disintegration of old worlds, but also the arising of new worlds. A philosophic approach towards apperception is needed within Futurism.

Where is one to seek out the vital sources behind the Futurist outlooks and Futurist currents in art? What has transpired within the world? Of what sort is the fact of being having begotten a new sense of life? There was some particular fateful moment in human history, the point from which there began to fall apart all the stability and crystaline aspect of life. The tempo of life has accelerated infinitely, and the whirlwind, caused by this accelerated pace, has seized hold and sent spinning both man and human creativity. Near-sightedly one would not have seen that in the life of mankind there has transpired a changing point, after which over the course of a decade there would happen such transformations, as earlier occurred only over the course of a century. In the old beauty of human existence and human art something from this critical moment radically collapsed, from this revolutionary event. Architecture tended to perish -- that finest expression of every organic artistic epoch. Modern architectural creativity is marked by the construction of enormous rail-stations and hotels. All the creative energy of man tends to go into the planning and construction of automobiles and aeroplanes, upon the discovery of means of accelerated transportation. The beauty of the old manner of life was static. The church, the palace, the rustic country-house -- were something static, they relied upon the stability of life and upon its slow tempo. Now however everything has become dynamic, everything statically stable is undone, swept up into the rapidity of mechanical motion. But a new dynamic style has not been fashioned, and there appears doubt of the possibility of the fashioning of such a style. Decadence was an initial stage of this process. But it was oriented backwards, in it there was a debilitating and total languor over the accepting of a process of life, destructive of beauty. The Decadents -- are aesthetes. Futurism -- is the final stage of this process, it seeks to be oriented forwards, in it is a delighted acceptance of this process of life, a total devoting of oneself to this process. And the Futurists -- are anti-aesthetic. What happened, where did it all come about from?

    The machine came out victoriously into the world and shattered the age-old harmony of organic life. This revolutionary event changed everything in human life, and it affected everything. It is impossible to sufficiently appreciate this event quite highly enough. Its enormous significance -- is not only social, but also cosmic. The growth of the importance of the machine and of the mechanical within human life tends to signify the entry into a new world aeon. The rhythm of organic flesh within world life has been broken. Life has been ripped away from its organic roots. Organic flesh has been replaced by the machine, in the mechanism is to be found the organic developement of its root. Machinisation and mechanisation -- are a fateful and inevitable cosmic process. It is impossible to hold back the old organic flesh from ruin. But only to the superficial glance does the machinisation represent materialisation, in the which spirit perishes. This process is not a transition from a more complex organic over to a simpler non-organic. At a deeper glance the machinisation has to be conceived of as a dematerialisation, as a pulverisation of the flesh of the world, a stretching apart of the material composition of the cosmos. The machine itself per se cannot kill spirit, it rather moreso enables the liberation of spirit from its bondage to organic nature. The machine is a crucifixion of the flesh of the world. Its victorious arrival betokens the eradication of all organic nature, it bears with it death to both plant and animal, to forests and flowers, to everything organic and by nature beautiful. The romantic grief over the perishing beautiful flesh of this world, for flowers, for trees, for pretty human bodies, beautiful churches, palaces and rustic dwellings is powerless to halt this fatal process. Thus is fulfilled the fate of the flesh of the world, it moves on towards the resurrection and to a new life through death. Futurism is a passive reflection of the machinisation, the disintegration and the crumbling of the old flesh of the world. The Futurists sing out about the beauty of the machine, they are delighted by its noise, and inspired by its movements. For them the charm of a motor has replaced the charm of a feminine body or flower. They are fascinated by the machine and the new sensations, connected with it. The miracle of electrification has replaced for them the miracle of divinely-beautiful nature. Other planes of being, concealed behind the physical trappings of the world, they do not know and do not want to know. The denial of other-worldliness -- is one of the points of the Futurist programme. And therefore they but reflect the process of disintegration on the physical plane. In their creativity they are open only to the splinters and chips of the old flesh of the world, they reflect a confusion of planes, not knowing the meaning of what is transpiring.

Only the spiritual apperceptivity of man can comprehend the transition from an old and disintegrating world to a new world. Only the creatively-active attitude of man to the elementally occurring process can beget a new life and a new beauty. The generation of the Futurists of every shade all too passively but reflect this elemental process. In such quite latest trends, as Suprematism, there is incisively posited the long since already considered task of an ultimate liberation of the pure creative act from the grip of the naturo-objective world. And the painting from a purely graphic element would have to recreate a new world, totally dissimilar to all the natural world. And in it there should have to be neither mature, with all its images, nor even man. This is not only a liberation of art from the here and now, this -- is a liberation from all the created world, a creativity propped up upon nothing. But is such a radicalism possible for the Futurist consciousness? I tend to think, that with the Futurists this is merely a powerless creative gesture and its significance but symptomatic. Futurism as regards its sense of life and its consciousness is nowise radical, it -- is merely a passing fancy, moreso the end of the old world, than the beginning of a new. The level of awareness of the Futurists remains superficial and it never penetrates down into the depths of the cosmic changes. They see only the surface level of what changes and stormy world movements are happening. That, what is occurring in the depths, remains hidden for them. They are too servilely dependent on the processes of the disintegration and stretching apart of the old flesh of the world, its material

THE CRISIS OF ART

trappings, in order for them to be able to create a new world not dependent upon the external process enslaving them. They are situated under the grip of the process of mechanisation, and their creativity is full of this machine-like objectness. They are liberated from the human bodies, from trees, from the seas and the hills, but they cannot liberate themselves from motors, from the electric light, from aeroplanes. But indeed this is likewise part of the object-oriented world. It is from this that the Futurists create, and not from the creative nothingness of the human spirit. The creative spirit is denied by them, they believe more in motors and electric lamps. The Futurists, given the condition of consciousness in which they are situated, create under the power of the motor and reflect the changes, wrought by the motor in world life. There is no wellspring of the dynamic with them. The Futurists are very shrill in their expressions, but in essence they are hopelessly unassuming and dependent upon the outward world. And to the Futurists must be opposed an immeasurably greater radicalism and creative daring, going out beyond the limits of this world. Passivity is powerless to contend against Futurism. To return to the old art, to the old beauty of the embodied world, to the classical norms, is impossible. The world has become disembodied in its trappings, reincarnated. And art cannot be preserved in its old embodiments. It has to create the new, the bodies not yet material, it has to carry over into another plane of the world. The true meaning of the crisis of the plastic arts -- is in the spasmodic attempts to penetrate beyond the material trappings of the world, to discern a more subtle flesh, to surmount the law of impenetrability, and this is a radical severing of art from antiquity. In the Christian world the Renaissance proved that everything is still possible, with its orientation towards antiquity. The forms of the human body have remained enduring. The human body -- is a thing of antiquity. The crisis of art, in which we are at present, is evidently a final and irreversible severing from all classicism.

Futurism obtains moreso in painting, than in literature. Literary Futurism has manifested itself most of all in manifestos. It is short on artistic creativity. There are a few poets of talent, and with them are some verses of talent. But a singularly noteworthy Futurist in artistic prose there is perhaps by name of Andrei Bely. He belongs to the generation of the Symbolists and he has always confessed a Symbolist faith. But in the artistic prose of A. Bely can be discerned images of an almost of genius

Futurist creativity.[1] This is to be sensed already in his symphonies. "With A. Bely there belongs uniquely to him an artistic sensing of a cosmic crumbling and stretching apart, a decrystalisation of all the things of the world, the breaking up and vanishing of all the firmly established boundaries between objects. With him the images themselves of people tend to get stretched and decrystalise, the borders get lost, such as separate one man from another and from the objects round about in his world. One man passes over into another man, one object passes over into another object, and the physical plane -- into the astral plane, the cerebral process -- into the existential process. There occurs a displacement and jumbling together of various planes. It began to seem to the hero of "Peterburg", that both he, and the room, and the objects in that room were re-embodied momentarily from objects of the real world into mentally-posited symbols purely logical in construct: the room dimensions became confused together with his lost awareness of body in the general existential chaos, termed by him *the universe*; the consciousness of Nikolai Apollonovich, separated from the body, became directly united with the electric light of the writing table, and termed "the sun of consciousness". This fragment can be termed totally Futurist as regards the expression in it of the sense of life. It is characteristic for A. Bely as a writer and an artist, that with him there begins a spinning about of words and interactive sounds and in this word-combination whirlwind that being itself tends to stretch, sweeping away all bounds. The style of A. Bely always in the final end passes over into a frantic circular motion. A. Bely sensed the whirlwind motion within cosmic life and found for it an adequate expression in his whirlwind word-combination. This -- is a direct expression in words of the cosmic whirlwinds. In the whirlwind intensification of word-combinations and sounds there obtains an increase of vital and cosmic intensity, an impulsion towards catastrophe. A. Bely stretches and pulverises the crystaline aspect of words, the solid forms of a word, seemingly eternal, and by this he expresses the stretching apart and pulverisation of the crystals within every thing of the objective world. The cosmic whirlwinds as it were break free and tear apart, pulverise all our settled and solid crystaline world. The creativity of A. Bely is also Cubism within an artistic prose, in style akin to

---

[1] On the same basis, by which I quoted from certain places in the article about Picasso, I here quote certain places from an article, concerning the "Peterburg" of A. Bely.

THE CRISIS OF ART

the painting Cubism of Picasso. With A. Bely there are torn loose whole veilings of the world's flesh, and for him there are no already yet salubrious organic images. In him there perishes the old, crystal-like beauty of the embodied world and there is born a new world, in which there is as yet no beauty. In the artistic prose of A. Bely everything likewise gets dislodged from its old, seemingly eternal place, just as with the Futurists. A. Bely belongs to a new era, when the integral perception of the image of man has been jolted, when man has gone through a fragmentation. He submerges man into the cosmic infinitude, betrays him to being torn apart by the cosmic whirlwinds. Lost are the boundary-lines, separating man from the electric lamp. There opens forth an astral world. The firm boundaries of the physical world have on the other hand safeguarded the independence of man, his particular firmly set boundaries, his crystaline features. The contemplation of the astral world, of this intermediate world betwixt spirit and matter, erases the boundaries, and decrystalises both man and the world surrounding him. All these whirlwinds -- are astral whirlwinds, and not whirlwinds of the physical world or of the humanly-emotional world". The Futurist world-sense and Futurist creativity of A. Bely radically is more distinct from other Futurists, in that it is connected for him with a great spiritual knowing, with a contemplation of other planes of being. From spiritual life A. Bely catches sight of a process of a cosmic disintegration and changing of all the cosmic order, and not from a dissolution itself of the materiality of the world. Here is why he detects a new cosmic rhythm, and in this is his virtue as an artist. The art of A. Bely is tormentive, it does not directly gladden, just as also with modern art. He does not permit of an artistic catharsis. But A. Bely moves on to other worlds, at a time when the Futurists in their blindness move on within an empty gaping void. It is necessary to admit of Futurism, to grasp its significance and move on to a new creativity. For this however there is inevitable a transition to another path, to another plane, outside that line, along which modern art is developing.

Art has to be free. This -- is an axiom very elementary, something not worth breaking a spear over. The autonomy of art has forever been affirmed. Artistic creativity ought not to be subjected to norms external to it, whether moral, social or religious. But the autonomy of art does not at all signify, that artistic creativity can or ought to be torn asunder from spiritual life and from the spiritual developement of man. Freedom is not a void. Free art emerges out from the spiritual depths of man, as a free fruition. And only profound and valuable is that art, in which there is sensed this depth. Art reveals freely all the depth and encompasses by itself all the fullness of being. But those, who are too frightened of heteronomous principles in art and its subordination to external norms, think to save the autonomy of art moreso, than they would by forcibly consigning it to an existence superficial and isolated. This is also what I tend to call spiritual illiteracy. A man, cast stranded on the surface, a man with an "I" disintegrated core, torn asunder into mere moments and shreds, cannot create powerful and great art. Art inevitably has to emerge from its shut-in and isolated existence and pass over to the creativity of a new life. And in this has to be admitted the truth of the synthetic strivings in art. Theurgy, about which have tended to dream the finest Symbolists and heralds of a religious art, -- represents the ultimate limit of human creativity. But the paths to theurgy are complex, tortuous and tragic. There is the danger of too prematurely and externally conceived a theurgic art. Art cannot and ought not to be subordinated to any sort of an external religious norm, to any sort of norm of spiritual life, which would transcend the art itself. By such a path would be created merely a tendentious art. In a truly however theurgic art the spiritual life of man would shine forth from within, and his religiosity would be but totally immanent. R. Wagner believed too much in the sacralness of the old culture, and V. Ivanov too much believes in this. Theurgic art in the strict sense of the word would be already an egress beyond the bounds of art as spheres of culture, as unique from cultural values, would be already a catastrophic passing over to the creativity of existence itself, of life itself. The path to it lies not through the safe-guarding of the old art and the old culture, not through a return to the past and not through a restoration of the sacral art of the ancient world and the Medieval world; the path to it lies through a sacrificial firmness of resolve to go forward through this process of fragmentation, distention and disintegration, the symptoms of which we see within Cubism and Futurism, and to survive this cosmic whirlwind with faith in the indestructibility of the creative spirit of man, of the core "I", called to creative work in the new world epoch. The Futurist machine aspect is but an external expression of a profound metaphysical process, an altering of all the cosmic harmony, begotten of a new cosmic rhythm, which proceeds from the depths. The new theurgic creativity, which is not something artistically to be anticipated, lies along another line, within the spiritual plane. When the new painters verymost current begin to set in their pictures newspaper

THE CRISIS OF ART

clippings and bits of glass, it runs along the line of a material dissociation to the point of an abject renunciation of creativity. At the end point of this process there begins to be a falling apart of the creative act itself whereby the creative daring gets replaced by a bold negation of creativity. Man is not a passive tool of the world process and of everything happening from its deterioration, he -- is an active creator. The cosmic pulling apart does not abolish the personal spirit, does not exterminate the "I" of man, if the human spirit makes an heroic effort to persevere and create within the new cosmic rhythm. The cosmic distention can only but enable a making apparent and reinforcing of the true core of the "I". The human spirit is being liberated from the old grip of organic matter. The machine with its claws tears out the spirit from the grip of matter, it destroys the old consolidating together of spirit and matter. In this -- is the metaphysical meaning of the appearance of the machine in the world. But the Futurists do not understand this. They situate themselves moreso on the perishing of matter, than on the liberating of spirit. The new art will create no longer still in the forms of physical flesh, but in the forms of another, a more refined flesh, it will pass over from material bodies to bodies soul-like.

The pathos of Futurism -- is the pathos of speed, a rapture of rapid movement. "We declare, that the magnificence of the world has been enriched by a new beauty: the beauty of speed". Thus declaims Marinetti. But speed is not something devised by the Futurists. The Futurists themself were created by the aspect of speed. The world indeed has entered into an era of rapid movement. But the Futurists conceive of and express merely the outward side of this rapidity of temporal motion. The inward motion, the inward speeding up as it were remains for the Futurists something hidden. But for a pervasive view it is clear, that the unprecedented motion and the unprecedented speeding up are begun within the depth of being and that the wellsprings of this motion and rapidness mustneeds be sought for within spiritual life. The apocalyptic prophecies speak about an accelerated aspect of time. The accelerated time, in which there develops an unprecedented and catastrophic motion, is an apocalyptic time. Futurism also can be conceived of as a phenomenon of apocalyptic time, although by the Futurists themselves this is something altogether inconceivable. But within apocalyptic time the greatest possibilities are combined with the greatest dangers. That which transpires with the world in all its spheres, is an apocalypsis of the whole enormous cosmic epoch, the end of the old world and the preliminaries of a new world. This is both more awesome and more abstract, than the Futurists themself realise. In the whirlwind jostling of the world, in the accelerated tempo of motion, everything gets dislodged from its place, breaking the material chains of old. But in this whirlwind there can perish also the greatest values, it can be, that man should not persevere, should be torn to shreds. There is possible not only the arising of a new art, but also the perishing of all art, of every value, of all creativity.

The present world war was initiated by Germany as a futuristic war. The Futurism from art passed over into life and in life gave more grandiose results, than within art. The futuristic exercises in conducting the war were prescriptions by Germany for all the world. The present war -- is a machine war. It -- to a remarkable degree is the result of the growing power of the machine within human life. This -- is an industrial war, in it the machine replaces man. The military might of Germany, now intimidating all the world, is a might first of all that is industrially mechanical, technical. In the present-day war the Futurists of the Marinetti type should be able to discern the new "magnificent world, the beauty of speed". The Futurist militarism has no respect for the great values of the old world, the old beauty, the old culture. We, as Russians, are least so the Futurists in this war, we are least so capable of its machine demands, its speed, its whirlwind motion, and we have most preserved both the old emotional virtues and the old emotional sins and vices. We are all given to being extensive, but not intensive. In this is the wellspring of our weakness. Within German militarism the futuristic machine aspect and the futuristic rapidity of movement have gotten to the point of supreme virtues, of frightening futuristic virtues. England and France strive to outstrip Germany in this, and they too make new discoveries. Thus the whole world is drawn into a military futuristic whirlwind. And the age-old barbarism of man, ingrained deeper than all culture, helps bring out this Futurism in life. But the sources of the world war, assuming such a futuristic guise, lie deeper, within the spiritual plane, where it begins and where it ends. In cosmic life indeed a spiritual war is being waged and a struggle made for the greatest values. And only by the spiritual war can mankind and the nations be saved for a new life. The material warfare is but a manifesting forth of the spiritual warfare. And all the whole task consists in this, that in this worldwide whirlwind there should be preserved the image of man, the image of a people and the image of mankind for an higher creative life. This task stands there in art, the same as this task stands there also in life.

THE CRISIS OF ART

It stands contrary to futuristic life and Futurist art. Its fulfilling cannot be attained by any sort of appeals to the past, nor by a safeguarding of this past. Futurism has to be passed through and surmounted both in life and in art. The surmounting is possible however through a deepening, through movement along a different measure, a measure of depth, and not along a flat plane, through knowledge, not abstract knowledge, but rather a living knowledge, cognitive-being.

We approach the final problem, which the crisis of art presents, a problem, which has tremendous significance for all our culture. I speak about the interrelationship of barbarity and decline. Human culture at its summits has an insurmountable tendency towards decline, towards decadence, towards an exhaustion. Such it was in the great culture of antiquity, which, essentially, is the eternal wellspring of all culture, and so also in the culture of the modern world. Culture constantly becomes separated from its vital and existential wellsprings, and at its summit it opposes itself to life, to being. There then ensues an epoch of late cultural decline, a very refined and beautiful culture. This -- is a beauty of fading blossoms, an autumnal beauty, knowing the greatest contradictions, losing its integral wholeness and spontaneity, but discovering a sagacious knowledge not only of itself, but also of that contrary to it. Epochs of cultural decline and cultural decay become likewise epochs of intensified awareness. Such epochs are to the utmost degree capable of an enfeebling, but also at the same time of an enriching of reflection, with a splintering and fragmenting, egressing beyond the borders of all organic givenness. Epochs of refinement and decline are not without fruition for the human spirit, and in them is its own glimmering of light. The decadence of culture makes for enormous proficiency and provides an opening ever so slightly to the unknowable. The typically impotent decadence can make assertions only from a certain delimited and relative point of view. But from a deeper point of view the decadence of the culture of antiquity, reaching the point of dead exhaustion, was profoundly fruitful and provided much for the spiritual life of the new, the Christian world. NeoPlatonism can be termed a philosophy of cultural decline for an entire world epoch. But NeoPlatonism played an enormously positive role in the spiritual life of mankind and plays it still also at present. Christianity was a salvific spiritual barbarism in regard to the cultural decline of the ancient world. But by mysterious paths the elements of decline passed over into this regenerating and renewing barbarity, without which the world would ultimately have perished. The barbarism of spirit and the barbarism of flesh and blood, welling up powers from the deepest dark wellsprings of being, drawing forth vigour from the dark roots of all life, from the not as yet enlightened nor transformed culturally unfathomable, in a mighty torrent had to flood upon human culture, when in it decline and exhaustion sets in. Christianity had to seem barbarism to the cultured peoples, such as were under the sway of the decline of the ancient world. And yet, this is but a limited pole of perspective. In actuality, Christianity was a revealing of light, drawn forth from the deepest depths of being, to which the ancient world had been unable to attain to. It was verymost a transformation of darkness into light, as ever the world did know. With the Gnostics there occurred a combining synthesis of all the old revelations of the ancient cultures together with the new Christian revelation from its depths of being. The Gnostics see not one thing only, but also another, they know in a light of wholeness and a light of disparateness, they unite together the revelations of "barbarism" and the revelations of "decadence". In this is the eternal sagacity of the Gnostic spiritual type. And this applies also for our era.

Every new culture in a fatal manner tends ultimately towards decline and exhaustion. The end of the XIX Century at its heights of culture generated the poisoned blossoms of decadence. These blossoms do not flower for long, they rapidly fade off. The Latin race, which also had produced the foundations of the old European culture, in which there was never any decisive breaking of its connections from antiquity, underwent a great stagnation, and in it ensued an exhaustion of vital powers. The French decadence was a final beautiful fruition of the cultural creativity of this great and very old race. The Germanic race in comparison with the Latin race was barbaric, in it there was not that ancient connection with antiquity, it had not those old traditions. In the culture, created by the Germans, there was a new depth, but there was not the subtle refinement nor the diversity, obtaining for the sagacity of a late setting. The Germans also were those barbarians, who once upon a time flooded upon Rome, upon the ancient world and renewed the blood of the old cultured races. With the Germanic race, having preserved in its blood even up to the present a certain barbarity, there is not so acutely the problem of the relationship of barbarism and decline, as with the Latin race. Oh, certainly, in German culture would be involved decadence in the process, and this is to be sensed in the present-day war. The whole of European culture at its

THE CRISIS OF ART

summits had to have sensed exhaustion and decay with having to seek out a reinvigoration of its powers in barbarity, which in our era is perhaps moreso inward, than outward, i.e. moreso deep a stratum of being, not yet transformed into culture. But world culture has gone out so far distant and so drained itself, that it cannot itself per se be of a strength for transforming that flood of darkness, which engulfs from the depths of being. At the summit heights of culture, which finds itself all more and more to be worldwide, there is discovered an ultimate barbarity. Culture is shewn to be but a very delicate layer. This is most of all perceived in the Latin race, the cradle of all European culture. Futurism had to have its birth in Italy, staggeringly bent beneath the weight of its own great cultural past, sapped of strength by this past greatness: Futurism likewise is a new barbarism upon the summits of culture. In it there is the barbarian coarseness, the barbarian wholeness and barbarian ignorance. This barbarism should have effected a change in the decline. But it transpired from a not very great depth. The culture is rending its own particular veils and discovers a not very deeply buried layer of barbarity, and here hence resound loudly the barbarian cries of the Futurist literature from the fissures, formed from the crisis of culture and art. And there is almost no hope, that the eternal normative culture, deriving its classical forms from antiquity, will vanquish these barbarian cries, these barbarian gestures. It begins to feel, that the trappings of culture, of the eternally classical culture, of the canonical culture, is sundered forever and cannot be reborn in the old sense of the word, which was always a return to antiquity. The sundering of the trappings of culture and the deep fissures in it is the symptom of a certain profound cosmic process. The world is changing its attire and trappings. Culture and art as an organic part of it is merely a set of attire of the world, merely the trappings of the world. I speak about the culture of which I am myself aware and construe as distinct from being, from life, and which sets itself in opposition to being, to life. Culture has transformed the initially given barbarian darkness of being into a certain bright realm, in which it has isolated itself and in which it takes pride as being self-sufficient. But culture in this its classical sense is not the sole path of the transformation of darkness into life, it is not the sole path of giving form to chaos. Through culture lies a path upwards and forward, not backwards, not to a pre-cultural condition, and this -- is the path of the transformation of culture itself into new bring, into a new heaven and a new earth. Only upon this path, bursting forth into culture, can the barbarian shouts and the barbarian gestures be harnessed to the new cosmic harmony and the new cosmic rhythm. Not only art, but all human creativity also will perish and plunge into the primordial darkness, if it does not become a creativity of life, a creativity of the new man and his spiritual path. The cultured and the decadent are situated in a condition of impotent fragmentedness, whereas the barbaric Futurists are situated in a condition of coarse wholeness and ignorance. For the new life, for the new creativity, for the new art there need to break through those Gnostics of the new type, who know the secret of integrality and the secret of dividedness, they know both the one and they know the other, opposite to it. Such a sagacious knowledge ought to help overcome the great conflict of barbarism and decline, which has many an expression, and which is but the manifestation moreso of the profound tragic conflict of the creativity of life and the creativity of culture. The emergence from this can be only through a passing over into a new world aeon, in the which all creativity would already become a continuation of God's Creation of the world. This transition is impossible to understand outwardly, and the inward understanding of the fate of art ought not to be transformed into a norm inwardly binding upon it. Art, just like all the spheres of culture, has to deal with its own existence and ultimately experience its own fate. In the world they will still create verses, pictures and musical symphonies, but in creativity the inner catastrophe will accelerate and from within glimmer through. Everything will turn out proportionate to the spiritual growth of man and the world. There exists now in world life however a variable growth and it is impossible from the outside and in terms of art to anticipate it. It has been said, that in the end-times people will get married and wed, will buy and trade. And in the upper spheres of cultural creativity much inwardly as it were remains as of old, inwardly however all will be engulfed by the flames. And those, who have sensed and have perceived the workings of these flames, bear a great responsibility and have to work at the spiritual regeneration of man and the inner enlightening of all his creative activity.

Picasso

(1914 - #174)[1]

When one enters into the Picasso room within the gallery of S. I. Schukin, one is seized with a feeling of subtle terror. That, what one senses, is connected not only with the painting and the fate of art, but with cosmic life itself and its fate. In the preceding room of the gallery was the charming Gauguin. And it seems, that one has experienced the ultimate joy of the natural life, the beauty all still of an embodied and crystaline world, the rapture of the natural rays of the sun. For Gauguin, the son of a refined and jaded culture, it was necessary to flee to the island of Tahiti, to exotic nature and to exotic people, in order to find in himself the strength to create the beauty of an embodied crystaline, sun-bright natural life. After this golden dream one is roused wide awake in the room of Picasso. Cold, gloomy, frightful. The delight of an embodied and sun-bright life has vanished. A wintry cosmic wind has torn away veil after veil, all the blossoms have faded, all the leaves, the skin of things is tripped away, all the coverings, all the flesh, manifest in forms of imperishable beauty, has fallen away. It seems, that never already will ensue a cosmic springtime, will not be the leaves, the greens, the beautiful veilings, the embodied synthetic forms. And if too there will be a springtime, then it will be totally different, new, unprecedented, with leaves and flowers not of here. It seems, that after the dreadful winter of Picasso the world will not blossom still, as before, that in this winter fall away not only all the veilings, but also that all the objective corporeal world is shattered apart down to its

---

[1] PIKASSO. First published in Journal "Sophiya", 1914, № 3, p. 57-62. Article was thereafter republished initially in Berdyaev 1918 anthology booklet of 3 articles, "Krizis iskusstva" ("The Crisis of Art") (Kl. № 14), Ch. 2. Article has also subsequently been reprinted in the Moscow "Liga" 1994 N. Berdyaev collection of articles, under cover-title, "Philosophiya, tvorchestva, kultury i isskustva", tom 2, ctr. 419-425.

foundations. There occurs as it were a mysterious stretching apart of the cosmos.

Picasso -- represents an expression of genius of the disintegration, the stretching apart and pulverisation of the physical, corporeal, embodied world. From the perspective of the history of painting, the *raison d'etre* for the arising of Cubism in France becomes understandable. Picasso was preceded as a painter by such immense figures, as Cezanne. French painting already for a long time, from the time of the Impressionists, had gone down the path of softening effects, had lost the sense of firm forms, down the path of the exclusively picturesque. Cubism is a reaction against this softening effect, a searching out of the geometric aspects of the objective world, of the skeleton of things. This -- is a matter of analytic, and not synthetic, searchings. All more and more it becomes impossible to have a synthetically-whole apperception and creativity in painting. Everything analytically decomposes and becomes dismembered. By suchlike an analytic dismemberment the painter gets down to the skeleton of things, to the firm forms, hidden behind the softening veils. The material veils of the world have begun to decompose and come apart and they have started to seek for the firm substances, congealed beyond this softened effect. In his searching for the geometric forms of objects, the skeleton of things, Picasso has arrived at the stone age. But this -- is an illusory stone age. The somberness, the frigidity and firmness of the geometric figures of Picasso only but seem so. In actuality, the geometric bodies of Picasso, piled up from the cubes of the skeleton of the corporeal world, fall apart at the slightest shake. The final layer of the material world, revealed by Picasso the painter after the stripping away of all the veils, -- is illusory, and not real. The insights of the painter do not reveal the substances of the material world, -- this world proves to be non-substantial. Picasso -- is a merciless exposer of the illusion of an embodied, materially synthetic beauty. Behind the captivating and alluring feminine beauty he sees the fear of disintegration, dissolution. He, as a seer, sees through all the veils, the garbs, the accretions, and there, in the depths of the material world, he sees his own heaped-up monstrosities. These -- are the demonic grimaces of the fettered spirits of nature. To go deeper even still, and there would not be any sort of materiality, -- there already would be the inner level of nature, of the hierarchy of spirits. The crisis in painting as it were leads to an emergence from the physical material flesh into another and higher plane.

THE CRISIS OF ART

Painting, as also with all the plastic arts, was an embodiment, a materialisation, a crystalisation. The higher ascents in the old painting provided a formal and crystaline flesh. And painting was connected with a solidity of the embodied physical world, with a stability of form with matter. But at present painting is undergoing an as yet unprecedented crisis. If one penetrates deeper into this crisis, then it is impossible to term it otherwise than as a *dematerialisation, a disembodiment of painting.* Within painting there is happening something, it would seem, contrary to the very nature of the plastic arts. It is as though everything already has been outlived within the sphere of the embodied, materially-crystaline painting. Art ultimately has torn itself loose from antiquity. There has begun a process of the permeation forth of painting beyond the limits of the material plane of being. In the old painting there was much of spirit, but of a spirit embodied and expressible within the crystals of a material world. Now there occurs a reverse process: spirit does not become embodied nor materialised, but rather matter itself becomes dematerialised, disembodied, it loses its firmness, its solidity, its stability of form. Painting plunges into the depths of matter and there, in the bottommost levels, it finds already no materiality. Were one to recourse to theosophic terminology, one might then say, that painting is effecting a transition from bodies physical to bodies aethereal and astral. Already within Vrubel [Mikhail, 1856-1910] there began a delicate distension of the material body. With Picasso there is a shakiness to the very boundaries of physical bodies. There is the same symptom with the Futurists, in their notices tempo of movement. The promotions and charlatanism, distorting the present-day art, have deep causes in the distortion of the crystaline aspect of everything vital. Already with the Impressionists began a sort of disintegrative process. And this is not from an immersion within spirituality, but occurs rather from an immersion in materiality. Early Italian painting was full of deep spirituality, but the spirit was embodied in it. In modern art spirit is as it were on the wane, and flesh becomes dematerialised. This is a very profound jolt for the plastic arts, and which strikes at the very essence of the plastic form. The dematerialisation in painting can produce the impression of the ultimate collapse of art. Painting just the same is bound up with the crystaline forms of flesh, as poetry is with the crystaline forms of the word. The dissociation of the word, its distention has to produce the impression of the collapse of poetry. And truly indeed there happens the same stretching apart of the crystaline aspects of words, as with the crystaline aspects of flesh. I shall not speak about the Futurist poetry, which up til now has produced nothing remarkable. But here too there is Andrei Bely, whom I regard as an original, remarkable, nigh close to genius phenomenon in Russian literature, who as such might be termed a Cubist within literature. In his novel "Peterburg" can be discerned the same process of stretching apart and pulling apart of cosmic life, which also is in the Picasso picture. In his belaboured and nightmarish word combinations there become distended the crystaline aspect of words. He is the same sort of vexing and nightmarish artist, as is Picasso. This painful vexation is from the stretching apart, from the ruination of the world, or more precisely, not of the world, but of one of the embodied worlds, one of the planes of world life.[1]

And it seems a sad and bitter thought, that there will no longer be beautiful bodies, pure crystals, the joys of embodied life, of the synthetically-whole apperception of things, of an organic culture. All this is passe, and the passe is discovered in aching grief, in sighs over the past, in painful fright at the perishing of the embodied beauty of the world. Architecture already has irreversibly gone to ruin, and its ruination is very noticeable and striking. With the perishing of the hope for the rebirth of a great architecture perishes also the hope of a new embodiment of beauty in an organic, naturo-corporeal national culture. In architecture a very shallow Futurism has long since already gained the victory. It would seem, that in the world of a material embodiment, of corporeality, everything is already crumbling irretrievably, everything is already *détraqué*. On this plane of being there has become impossible already any organic, synthetically-integral joy, any stability of beauty. It would seem, that in nature itself, in its rhythm and cycles something irreversibly has crumbled and changed. There is no longer and cannot be such a pretty Springtime, such a sunny Summer, nor the crystaline aspect, the purity, the clarity, in either the Springtime or in the Summer. The times of the year are all mixed up.

---

[1] In philosophy Cubism also is possible. Thus, the critical genealogy in its final results arrives at a distortion and disintegration of being. In the Russian philosophy of the present time as a genuine Cubist there appears to be B. V. Yakovenko [1884-1949]. His philosophy is a pluralistic dissegmentation of being. Vide his 1910 article in "Logos". And it is characteristic, that in Germany already there has appeared a work, suggesting a parallel between Picasso and Kant.

THE CRISIS OF ART

People no longer rejoice at the rising and the setting of the sun, as formerly they were wont to rejoice. The sun itself no longer shines as before. In nature itself, in the meteorological and geological phenomena there is occurring a mysterious process of an analytic dissociation and distention. Many perceptive people now feel this, such as are endowed with a mystical sensitivity towards cosmic life. About human life, about the human being, about the human social aspect there is nothing to say. Here everything is clearly visible, evident. Our life is a continuous decrystalisation, dematerialisation, disembodiment. The successes of material technology only but enable the disintegration of historical bodies, of the orderly manner of flesh born in life. All the stability is shaken, and with it is shaken not only the past evil and injustice of life, but also the past beauty and past comfort in life. The material world seemed to be absolutely stable, firmly crystalised. But this stability has proven to be but relative. The material world is not substantial -- it is merely functional. And already outmoded are those conditions of spirit, which engendered this sense of stability and crystalising aspect of the embodied material world. Now at present the human spirit is entering into another stage of growth in its being and the symptoms of the distention and dissolution of the material world can be seen everywhere: both in the jolts to traditional lifestyle and all our way of life, to kindred bonds, and in science, which snatches away the traditional boundaries of experience and is compelled to admit of a dematerialisation, and also in philosophy, and in art, and in the occult currents, and in the religious crisis. There is decomposing the old synthesis of an objective world of things, there perishes irretrievably the crystals of the old beauty. But the attainment of beauty, which would have corresponded to another stage of growth for man and the world, there is not still. Picasso -- is a remarkable painter, profoundly agitating, but in him there is no attainment of beauty. He is all transitional, all -- crisis.

It would be onerous, pitiful and painful to live in such a time for a man, who loves exclusively the sun, clarity, Italy, the Latin genius, the embodiment and crystalising aspect. Such a man would experience immeasurable sorrow over the irretrievable perishing of everything valuable within the world. And only in the depths of spirit could he find an antidote against this terror and discover a new joy. In German culture this crisis is sensed less, since the German culture always was too exclusively of spirit and did not know of such an embodied beauty, of such a crystalisation within matter. The world is changing its veils. The material veilings of the world were but a temporary attire. The old leaves and blossoms had to fade under the cosmic wind. The old clothes of being rot and fall away. This -- is a sickness in the maturing process of being. But being is indestructible in its essence, not disintegrative at its core. Within the process of the cosmic crumbling of the clothes and veilings of being both man and everything genuinely existent has to persevere. Man, as the image and likeness of absolute being, cannot crumble away. But he is subject to the dangers of the cosmic whirlwinds. He ought not to surrender himself to the capricious whims of the wind. In the artistry of Picasso there is no longer man. That, which he uncovers and reveals, is already no longer human; he surrenders man to the whims of the crumbling wind. But the pure crystal of the human spirit is indestructible. It is only that modern art is powerless to create crystals. At present we approach not a crisis within painting, of which there have been many, but rather a crisis of painting in general, of art in general. This -- is a crisis of culture, an awareness of its failure, its impossibility to transform itself into a culture of creative energy. The cosmic distention and disintegration engender a crisis of all the arts, jolting the boundaries of art. Picasso -- is a vivid symptom of this sickened process. But such symptoms are many. In front the pictures of Picasso I tended to think, that with the world was transpiring something inharmonious, and felt sorrow and grief at the perishing of the old beauty of the world, but then too joy at the birth of the new. This is a great praise to the power of Picasso. The same thoughts occur with me, when I read occult books, and communicate with people, living in this sphere of phenomena. But I believe, I believe deeply, that there is possible a new beauty within life itself and that the perishing of the old beauty merely seems so to us in regard to our limitedness, and because, that all beauty -- is eternal and present at the deepest core of being. And the debilitating sorrow has to be surmounted. If one say it as a truth less than ultimate, that the beauty of Botticelli and Leonardo is perishing irretrievably together with the perishing of the material plane of being, upon which it was embodied, then as an ultimate truth one ought to say, that the beauty of Botticelli and Leonardo has entered into eternal life, since it always has abided beyond the unstable veiling of cosmic life, to which we give the name material. But the new creativity will be yet different, it will not be yet cut short by the pull to the gravity of this world. Picasso -- is not the new creativity. He -- is the end of the old.

An Astral Novel

(Reflections on A. Bely's Novel "Peterburg")

(1916 - 233)[1]

I.

Peterburg no longer exists. The life of this city was a bureaucratic life predominantly, and its end was a bureaucratic end. What has arisen is the unfamiliar and to our ears still strange sounding Petrograd. There has ended not only an old word and in its place arisen a new word, there has ended an entire historical period, and we find ourselves entering upon a new and unknown period. There was something strange and terrible in the rise of Peterburg, in its fate, in its relationship to the whole of enormous Russia, in its being torn off from the life of the people, something at once both powerfully enervating and phantasmic. By the magic volition of Peter, Peterburg rose up from out of nothing, from the marshy mists. Pushkin gave us a feel of the life of this Peterburg in his "Bronze Horseman". The earthy Slavophil Dostoevsky was a peculiar example connected with Peterburg, far moreso than with Moscow, and he revealed in it the irrational Russian element. The heroes of Dostoevsky were primarily

---

[1] ASTRAL'NYI ROMAN (Razmyshlenie po povodu romana A. Belogo "Peterburg"). First published in Journal "Birzhevye vedomosti", 1 July 1916, № 15608. Republished initially in 1918 Berdyaev's anthology text of 3 articles, "Krizis iskusstva" ("The Crisis of Art"), Ch. 3.

Article reprinted also in 1989 YMCA Press Tom 3 of Berdyaev's writings, -- "Tipy religioznoi mysli v Rossii", p. 430-440.

Article has also appeared subsequently in several Russian collections of Berdyaev articles such as the Moscow "Vyshaya shkola" 1993 text, "O russkikh klassikakh", p. 310-317; and also the Moscow "Liga" 1994 text, "Philosophiya, tvorchestva, kultury i isskustva", Tom 2, p. 438-446.

Nicholas Berdyaev

Peterburg heroes, connected with the Peterburg damp and mist. It is possible to find in him remarkable pages about Peterburg, about its phantasmic quality. Raskol'nikov strolled about Sadova and the Senna haymarket, plotting his crime. Rogozhin committed his crime at Gorokhova. The earthy Dostoevsky loved groundlessly unstable heroes, and only in the atmosphere of Peterburg could they exist. Peterburg, in contrast to Moscow, -- is a catastrophic city. Characteristic likewise are the tales of Gogol, -- in them is a Peterburg horror. To the Moscow Slavophils Peterburg seemed a foreign and alien city, and they were afraid of Peterburg. There was a large reason for this, since Peterburg -- was the eternal threat to the Moscow Slavophil well-being. But that Peterburg should seem an altogether non-Russian city, this was due to their provincial lack of insight, their limitedness. Dostoevsky made up for this lack of insight.

The ephemeral quality of Peterburg, -- is purely a Russian ephemeral quality, a phantasm, created by the Russian imagination. Peter the Great was Russian right down to the very marrow of his bones. And the Peterburg bureaucratic style itself -- is a peculiar offspring of Russian history. The German engrafting onto the Peterburg bureaucracy creates the specific Russian bureaucratic style. This is true, in the same way that the characteristic French language of the Russian nobility is a Russian national style, just as Russian, as is the Russian empire-style. The Peterburg Russia is our other national image alongside the image of Muscovite Russia.

A novel about Peterburg can only be written by a writer, endowed with an altogether special feeling of cosmic life, a feeling of the ephemeral quality of being. We have such a writer, and he has written the novel "Peterburg", he has written it just before the very end of Peterburg and the Peterburg period of Russian history, as though a summation of our quite strange capital and its strange history. In the novel "Peterburg", perhaps the most remarkable Russian novel since the time of Dostoevsky and Tolstoy, it is impossible to find it in its totality, not all Peterburg has found its place therein, not everything has found access to the author. But something characteristic of Peterburg was genuinely grasped and reproduced in this novel. This -- is an artistic creation of the Gogol type, and therefore can occasion the accusation of a slander against Russia, with its exclusive acceptance of the monstrous and the ugly, and in it is difficult to find man, in the image and likeness of God. Andrei Bely -- is a most remarkable Russian writer of the latest literary era, very original, creating a completely

THE CRISIS OF ART

new form in artistic prose, a completely new rhythm. To our shame he is still insufficiently recognised, but I do not doubt, that with time there will be recognised his genius, impaired and incapable for the creation of perfective works, but striking by its new feeling of life and by its no longer still former musical form. A. Bely will be installed amidst the ranks of the Russian great writers, as genuinely continuing Gogol and Dostoevsky. Such a place has already been assured for him by his novel, "The Silver Dove". A. Bely has to him a certain inner rhythm present, and as felt by him he is in accord with a new cosmic rhythm. These artistic revelations of A. Bely have found their expression in his symphonies, in a form, not yet met with in literature. The appearance of A. Bely in art can be compared only with the appearance of Scriabin. It is not by chance, that both for the one and for the other there is a gravitation towards theosophy, towards occultism. This is connected with the sensation of the onset of a new cosmic epoch.

II.

With A. Bely, and belonging only to him, is an artistic feeling of cosmic expanse and atomisation, a decrystalisation of all the things of the world, the breaking down and disappearance of all he firmly established boundaries between objects. The very forms of people for him decrystalise and atomise, they lose the firm boundaries, which separate one man from another and from the objects of the surrounding world. The firmness, the limitedness, the crystalisation of our fleshly world is demolished. One man passes over into another man, one object passes over into another object, the physical plane -- passes over into the astral plane, the cerebral process -- passes over into the existential process. There occurs a mixing and shifting of various planes. The hero of "Peterburg", the son of an important bureaucrat, a Cohenite and revolutionary, Nikolai Apollonovich, has locked himself in with a key in his work room: it then begins to seem to him, that both he, and the room, and the objects of this room have become reincarnated instantly from objects of the real world into mentally-posited symbols of purely logical constructs: the room's expanse mixes itself up with his lost bodily sensation into a general existential chaos, termed by him as universal; the consciousness of Nikolai Apollonovich, having become separate from the body, immediately unites itself with the electric lamp on his writing table, termed "the sun of consciousness". Locked in, and reasoning the position of his step after step as a system brought into unity, he sensed his own body effused throughout the "universe", i.e. the room; the head of this body shifts itself into the head of the glass of the electric lamp under the coquettish lampshade. Herein is described the meditation of Nikolai Apollonovich, by means of which his peculiar being disintegrates. Beyond this lies hidden the artistic contemplation of A. Bely himself, and in the contemplation of this there splinters both his own particular nature and the nature of all the world. The boundaries are demolished, separating the ephemeral from the actual, and in "Peterburg" everything is a cerebral interplay of the important bureaucrat father, the senator, the head of an institute and virtually privy-counselor Apollon Apollonovich Ableukhov, only with difficulty distinguished from his son the revolutionary, the bureaucrat turned inside out, Nikolai Apollonovich. It is difficult to determine, where the father ends and where the son begins. These enemies, representing opposite principles -- the bureaucratic and the revolutionary, mix together into a sort of uncrystalised, unformed whole. In this similarity, the mixing together and the demolishing of boundaries there is symbolised also this, that our revolution is flesh from flesh and blood from blood of the bureaucracy, and that therefore within it is lodged the seed of decay and death.

Everything passes over into everything, everything is jumbled together and becomes indistinct. The features of established being dissipate. For A. Bely, as a writer and an artist, it is characteristic of him always that there begins a spinning around of words and sounds together and in this whirlwind of word-combination being itself becomes pulverised, all the boundaries shift. The style of A. Bely always in the end finally passes over into a frenzied spinning motion. In his style there is something of the Khlysty element. A. Bely has perceived this whirling motion to be in cosmic life and has found for it an adequate expression in a whirlwind of word-combination. The language of A. Bely is not a translation into some other, some foreign language of his cosmic life impressions, as we thus see in the beautifully helpless painting of Ciurlionis. This -- is a direct expression of cosmic whirlwinds in words. To reproach him is possible only with his insufferable style, for he often goes astray. The genius of A. Bely as an artist -- is in this coincidence of a cosmic shifting and cosmic whirlwind with a verbal shifting, with the whirlwind of word-combination. In the whirlwind the intensity of word and sound combinations is given intensity by a vital and cosmic tension, pulling towards catastrophe. A. Bely stretches and pulverises the crystaline aspect of words, the firm forms of words, seemingly eternal, and by this he expresses the stretching and pulverisation of the crystaline aspects of everything, the object in the world. The cosmic whirlwinds as it were uproot and expose to freedom, they pulverise everything of our established, firm-set, crystaline world. "The world fabric constituted a fabric of furor". With these words A. Bely finely characterises the atmosphere, in which the action of "Peterburg" takes place. And here is how the city of Peterburg presents itself to him: "Peterburg, Peterburg! Besieged by fog, and me thou hast pursued with the frivolity of a cranial game: thou -- art a cruel-hearted tormentor; thou -- art an unsettling apparition; thou, aforetime, for years hath assaulted me; I fled upon thine frightsome prospekts and at a run I flew up Chuguna to that bridge, beginning with the outer land, leading to boundless expanse; beyond the Neva, into the half-light, thine green remoteness -- arise with phantoms of islands and houses, enveloped in the vain hope, that this border is actuality, and that it -- be not a belligerent infinity, which should banish upon the Peterburg street the miserable wisp of the clouds".

III.

A. Bely can be termed a Cubist in literature. Formally he can compare with Picasso in art. The Cubist method -- is the method of an analytic, and not synthetic, perception of things. Cubism in art seeks after the geometric skeleton of things, it demolishes the deceptive coverings of flesh and strives to penetrate into the inner structure of the cosmos. In the Cubist art, Picasso destroys the beauty of the embodied world, everything decomposes and stratifies. In a precise sense there is no Cubism in literature. But there is possible therein something analogous and parallel to the Cubism in painting. The creativity of A. Bely is also a Cubism in artistic prose, in strength akin to the Cubist painting of Picasso. For A. Bely also, the wholistic coverings of world flesh are demolished, and for him there are already no integral organic forms. The Cubist method of the disintegration of every organic being is applied by him to literature. Here there cannot be spoken anything about the influence upon A. Bely of the Cubism in painting, with which he, in all probability, is little familiar. His Cubism is his own particular, original apperception of the world, so characteristic for our transitory era. In a certain sense A. Bely -- is a singularly genuine, remarkable futurist within Russian literature. Within him perishes the old, crystaline beauty of the embodied world and a new world is born, in which there is no longer beauty. In the artistic manner of A. Bely everything thus is shifted from its own old, seemingly eternal place, as also with the Futurists. He does not write agitational manifestos, he writes rather other and symbolic manifestos, but in his essence and by his creativity he destroys all the old forms and creates new ones. The originality of A. Bely is in this, that he combines his Cubism and Futurism with a genuine and unmediated Symbolism, at the same time as the Futurists customarily and with hostility contrast themselves to the Symbolists. Thus in the Cubist-Futurist "Peterburg" the everywhere appearing red domino is an excellent, inwardly begotten symbol of revolutionary effort, essentially unreal. Within European literature a predecessor to the creative mannerisms of A. Bely might be considered Hoffmann [E.T.A., 1776-1822] in whose ingenious fantasy likewise all the boundaries become abolished and all planes transposed, everything is twofold and passes into its other. In Russian literature, A. Bely represents a direct continuation of Gogol and Dostoevsky. Just like Gogol, he sees in human life moreso the monstrous and the terrible, than rather beauty and authentically firm being. Gogol perceived the already old organically-whole world analytically and dissectively, for him the image of man is stretched and pulverised, and he saw the monsters and the astonishing in the depths of life, which otherwise Picasso has revealed in painting. Gogol has broken asunder from Pushkin, from the eternally beautiful and harmonious world-sense and world-outlook. And thus too it is with A. Bely.

But it is impossible not to reproach him on this, that in "Peterburg" he at places too much copies Dostoevsky, he is in too great a dependence on the "Possessed". Certain scenes, for example, the scene in the inn, there also is too direct a copying from the manner of Dostoevsky. And in these places A. Bely goes astray with another, a style not his own, and he destroys the rhythm of his own novel-symphony. He inwardly is connected with Dostoevsky, and for this it is impossible to reproach him, but he ought to have been more free in his artistic mannerisms, more assured in his own particular style. There is a great difference between A. Bely and Dostoevsky, they belong to different epochs. A. Bely is more cosmic as regards his feeling of life, Dostoevsky is more psychological and anthropological. To Dostoevsky was revealed the abyss in the depths of man, but the image of man was separated for him from the abyss of cosmic life. Dostoevsky perceived man as organically whole, he always saw the image of God in man. A. Bely belongs to a new epoch, when the integral perception of the image of man is shaken, when man undergoes fragmentation. A. Bely plunges man into the cosmic infinitude, he surrenders him to the rending of the cosmic whirlwinds. The boundary is lost, separating man from the electric light. There is disclosed an astral world. The firm boundaries of the physical world have protected from the opposite side the independence of man, his own firm boundaries, his crystal sketchings. The contemplation of the astral world, of this mid-point world between spirit and matter, erodes the boundaries, decrystalises both man, and his surrounding world. A. Bely -- is an artist of the astral plane, into which unnoticed slips our world, losing its own firmness and form. All these whirlwinds -- are astral whirlwinds, and not the whirlwinds of the physical world or the world of the human soul. "Peterburg" -- is an astral novel, in which everything goes out beyond the limits of the physical flesh of this world and the soul-life form of man, everything tumbles into the abyss. The senator sees already two expanses, and not one.

IV.

A. Bely artistically reveals the unique metaphysics of the Russian bureaucracy. Bureaucratism -- is an ephemeral being, a cerebral exercise, in which everything is composed of straight lines, of cubes of squares. Bureaucratism administers Russia from the centre according to the geometric method . The phantasm of the bureaucracy begets also the phantasm of revolution. It is not by chance that Nikolai Apollonovich is rendered a Cohenite,[1] i.e. as regards his philosophic trend he has no sense of the reality of being, and it is not by chance that he is connected by blood with the bureaucracy. All the way up to the ephemeral, the withdrawn astral plane of "Peterburg", nothing reaches from the depths of Russia, from the bosom of the life of the people. The centralism of the revolutionary committee is just as ephemeral a being, as is the centralism of the bureaucratic department. The process of rottenness has passed over from bureaucratism to revolutionism. The provocation, the dense mist that

---

[1] *trans. note*: a follower of the Neo-Kantianism of Hermann Cohen.

the revolution is wrapped up in, discloses its illusory-ephemeral character -- everything is transformed into Satanic whirlwinds.

    A. Bely is not altogether an enemy of the revolutionary idea. His point of view is not at all that, which Dostoevsky had in the "Possessed". The evil of the revolution for him was begotten by the evil of the old Russia. In essence, he wants artistically to unmask the phantasmic character of the Peterburg period of Russian history, of our bureaucratic Westernism and our Intelligentsia Westernism, similar to how in his work, "The Silver Dove" he unmasked the darkness of the Eastern element in the life of our people. In the capacity of his artistic talent, A. Bely, just like Gogol, was not called to reveal and reproduce the positive, the bright and the pretty. A. Bely in one of his verses calls on his Russia, beloved by him with a strange love, that it should scatter itself into the expanse. And from his novels, written about Russia, there remains he impression, that Russia should fly off into space, transform itself into star dust. He loves Russia with an annihilative love and he believes in its rebirth only through its perishing. Such a love is peculiar to the Russian nature.

    Everything phantasmic -- the bureaucratic, the revolutionary and the Kantian-gnosseological -- comes together in Nikolai Apollonovich. But within him the author shows still one terror. From Vl. Solov'ev, A. Bely inherited the terror afront the Mongol threat. And he senses the Mongol element within Russia itself, within the Russian man. Nikolai Apollonovich, just like his father, the head of a department, -- is a Mongol, a tyrant. The Mongol principle governs Russia. The Mongol East reveals itself in even the Russian West. The tyrant-Mongol principle glimmers for A. Bely even within Kantianism. A. Bely depicts the end of Peterburg, its final disintegration. The Bronze Horseman has played its way out into the Peterburg man. The image of the Bronze Horseman dominates the atmosphere of "Peterburg" and everywhere dispatches its astral double.

V.

    A. Bely has no Russian ideology, and it is unnecessary to seek for one in him. Rather than a Russian ideological consciousness, his is moreso a Russian nature, Russian element, and he -- is Russian to the depths of his being, within him the Russian chaos stirs. His sundering from Russia is something external and only seems to be so, just as with Gogol. A. Bely both loves Russia, and denies Russia. Just indeed as Chaadaev also loved

THE CRISIS OF ART

Russia. Not so altogether long ago A. Bely published a verse, in which are the following lines:

> My country! My native country!
> I -- am thine! I -- am thine!
> Accept me, weeping and not knowing
> The cut of damp grass...

    This verse finishes off with a confession of faith, that beyond the Russian "night" -- is "He". He, -- is Christ, beyond the terrible darkness and chaos of Russia. As regards himself, A. Bely knows, how terrible, how fearsome, how threatening the Russian chaos is. But he lacks the strength to waken in himself the Russian will, the Russian consciousness. He seeks entirely in the West for the discipline of will and consciousness. And it is possible to doubt, that he will find it there. I think, that he will turn round ultimately to Russia and in the depths of Russia he will seek the light.

    In "Peterburg" there are great artistic deficiencies, and much that is aesthetically unacceptable. The style of the novel does not hold up, the ending is too opportune, inwardly disconnected, and in places there is too great a dependence on Dostoevsky. But the nature of the artistic genius of A. Bely also cannot create an artistically perfect product. In his artistic creativity there is no catharsis, there is always something tormentive, since he himself as an artist does not arise above those elements, which he depicts, he does not surmount them, he himself is immersed in the cosmic whirlwind and dissolution, he himself is in the nightmare. In his novel there is not only no ideological way, no conscious way out, but there is also no artistic and catharsic exit, he does not set free, he remains within the grip of the nightmare. He oversteps the bounds of art of the perfective and the beautiful. His art is his own being, his chaos, his whirling motion, his cosmic sensation. And this is new and unusual in him. This mustneeds be accepted without seeking for consolation. It is impossible to approach him in the old critical ways. He is an artist of a passive cosmic epoch. And he anew returns literature to the great themes of the old Russian literature. His creativity is connected with the fate of Russia, with the Russian soul. He is the first to have written truly an astral novel, so dissimilar to the weak and unartistic occult novels, written in the old modes. A. Bely -- is not theurgic, but theurgic art perhaps will find itself on the path of the astral extension and disintegration in the creativity of his type.

Addenda

The Ivanov Wednesdays

(1916 - 55,1)[1]

In the autumn of 1905 Vyacheslav Ivanovich Ivanov and his now deceased wife, Lydia Dmitrievna Zinov'eva-Annibal, arranged for themself at the "Towers", -- their so-called quarters at the Tauride located on the ninth floor, -- to have open-house Wednesdays. At first these were modest gatherings of friends and close acquaintances from the literary world. The Ivanovs had not before transferred to Petrograd from abroad and had made literary connections. But somehow they happened at once to create around them a special atmosphere and to attract people of the most varied inner views and trends. This was an atmosphere of an especial graciousness, congenial, and quite lacking in any spirit of boorishness or exclusivity. V. I. Ivanov and L. D. Zinov'eva-Annibal were truly endowed with a gift of communicating with people, a gift of attracting people and bringing them mutually together. They expended much by way of a talent of energy with people, they devoted much attention to each man, they took interest in each separately and they interested each themself, included them into their own atmosphere, into the circle of their searchings. It immediately however became apparent, that V. I. Ivanov was not only a poet, but also erudite, a thinker of mystical outlook, a man of very broad and varied interests. What always impressed me about Vyach. Ivanov was this extraordinary capacity to talk with each person upon those themes, with which they were most of all interested in -- with the student about his discipline of study, with the artist about painting, with the musician about music, with the actor about the theatre, with the societal activist about societal questions. But this was not a mere accommodating of people, not a mere glibness and plasticity,

---

[1] IVANOVSKIE SREDY. Article originally appeared in the three volume 1914-1916 anthology compiled by S. A. Vengerov entitled, "Russkaya literatura XX veka", Moscow, publisher Mir -- in the 1916 Tom 3 issue, p. 97-100.
Reprinted since in the sbornik-anthology of N. Berdyaev articles under the title, "Mutnye liki (Tipy religioznoi mysli v Rossii)", Publisher "Kanon+", Moskva, 2004, ctr. 123-127.

not a mere fashionable worldliness, which in V. Ivanov was truly stupendous, -- this was likewise the gift of imperceptibly including each into the atmosphere of his own interests, his own themes, his own poetical or mystical experiences through a path, which each proceeds upon in life. V. Ivanov never stirred up any sort of discords, nor got into sharp disputes, he always sought to bring together and unite various people and varied trends, he loved to work out common platforms. He masterfully came up with questions, and from disparate people he provoked avowals intimate and of idea. Always it was the wish of V. Ivanov to transform the gathering of people into a Platonic Symposium, always he invoked Eros. "Sobornost'" -- was a fond slogan if his. All these traits were very favourable for the formation of a centre, a spiritual laboratory, in which clashed and were formulated various currents literary and of idea. And soon the Wednesday "at-homes" were transformed into events for all Petrograd, and even not Petrograd alone, -- these were the "Ivanov Wednesdays", around which accumulated whole legends. The number of people visiting on wednesdays all tended to increase, and the talks became systematically planned ahead, with a chairman, and with definite themes. The true soul and heart of the "Ivanov Wednesdays" was L. D. Zinov'eva-Annibal. She did not speak all that much, was not given to opinions and ideas, but she created an atmosphere of gracious femininity, which enabled the flow of our conversation and gatherings. L. D. Zinov'eva-Annibal was of altogether of different a nature, than Vyach. Ivanov, who was more Dionysian, emotional, impetuous, revolutionary in temperament, elemental, eternally pushing forward and upwards. Such a woman's touch in combination with the refined academism of Vyach. Ivanov, who was too much involved and self-contained in scope, and arduously caught up in his singular and ultimate faith, tended to form a talented and poetically rendered atmosphere of interaction, no one and in nothing spurning nor repulsing anyone. The "Wednesdays" continued for three years, answering a brewing cultural need, during which time everything was going to pieces and undergoing various changes. And I, so it seems, did not miss a single "Wednesday" and was invariably a chairman at all the resulting talking.

At the "Ivanov Wednesdays" were to be met people of very varied gifts, positions and trends. Mystical anarchists and the Orthodox, decadents and academic professors, neo-Christians and Social Democrats, poets and scholars, artists and thinkers, actors and social activists -- all peacefully came together at the Ivanov Towers and peacefully conversed on themes literary, artistic, philosophical, religious, occult, on the literary evil of the day and on the final, the ultimate problems of being. But there prevailed a tone and style mystical. And right off there was created an atmosphere, in which it was very easy to speak. In the setting of themes and in the character, in which they were put forth for consideration, perhaps, there was no grasping with a vital edge, and no one tended to think, that the discourse concerned his most vital interests. But there was formed a refined cultural laboratory, a place for the meeting of various currents of idea, and this was a fact, imbued with significance within our intellectual and literary history. Much was conceived and spouted forth in the atmosphere of these conversations. Mystical anarchism, mystical realism, Symbolism, occultism, neo-Christianity, -- all these trends were addressed on the Wednesdays, they had their own chairmen. The themes, connected with these currents, always were presented for conversation. But it would be a mistake to regard the Wednesdays, as religio-philosophic gatherings. This was not a place of religious searchings. This was a sphere of culture, of literature, but with a tendency towards the extreme. Mystical and religious themes were presented moreso as themes cultural and literary, than of vital matters of life. Many approached religious themes from the aspect of the historico-cultural, the aesthetic, the archeological. Mysticism was a novelty for the Russian cultural people, and in the approach towards it was a sense of insufficient experience and knowledge, too literary an attitude towards it. This was a time of spiritual crisis and fracturing of ideas in Russian society, in its most cultured level. At the "Wednesdays" came people, grouped around journals with new an outlook -- such as "The World of Art", "The New Path", "Questions of Life", "The Balance Scales". The level of our aesthetic culture was raised, there was ignited an awareness of the tremendous significance of art for a Russian Renaissance. And all at once the Russian literary-artistic movement became intertwined with the religio-philosophic. In the person of Vyach. Ivanov both currents were melded into a single image, and this intertwining of various sides of Russian spiritual life was all the time to be sensed at the "Wednesdays". But there was nothing of the narrow clique, of the sectarian mindset. At the talks one found one's own spot alongside people of different a spirit, positivists, loving poetry, and Marxists with a taste for literature. I remember a talk on Eros, one of the central themes of the "Wednesdays". A genuine symposium was formed, and speeches on love were pronounced by such varied people, as the host himself Vyacheslav Ivanov, and there was Andrei Bely having arrived from Moscow and then too the refined Prof. F. F. Zelinsky, and A. Lunacharsky -- seeing in the modern proletariat a reincarnation of the ancient Eros, and also a certain materialist, who acknowledged nothing to it save for physiological processes. But there prevailed the Symbolists and philosophers of religious an outlook. Frequent visitors and participants on the Wednesdays were E. Anichkov, M. Voloshin, L. Gabrilovich, Prof. F. Zelinsky, Vyach. G. Karatygin, Prof. N. Kotlyarevsky, V. Meierhol'd, V. Nuvel', Prof. M. Rostovtsev, F. Sologub, G. Chulkov, K. Siunnerberg. Often there came, though less frequently tending to speak -- A. Blok, Bakst, Dobuzhinsky, S. Gorodetsky, M. Kuzmin, K. Somov, A. Remizev, P. Solov'eva. More rarely to be encountered were D. Merezhkovsky, Z. Gippius, D. Filosofov, A. Kartashev, and likewise V. Rozanov. Wednesdays not infrequently were devoted to poetry, and many a young poet first read their verses there. The Wednesday gatherings gradually began to expand, and there appeared all more and more new people. In Petrograd there was a great deal of talk about the "Ivanov Wednesdays", and interest in it was evoked in various circles, sometimes far removed. At one of the Wednesdays, when there was a gathering of men comprising about 60 poets, painters, artists, thinkers, the erudite, all peacefully conversing on refined cultural themes, suddenly there appeared an official from the Okhrana secret-police department with a whole detachment of soldiers, who with their rifles and bayonettes took up position around all the doorways. For almost the entire night the search dragged on, with the result that the unexpected guests had to admit their mistake. This was the night that there also vanished the cap of Merezhkovsky, who then wrote an article on this theme in the newspapers. Politics at the Wednesdays there was not, despite the tumult of revolution all around. But the Dionysian societal atmosphere was reflected at the "Wednesdays". In a different era the "Wednesdays" would not have been possible. In the third year of existence the Wednesday gatherings began to go into decline, they lost their intimate character and got to be quite crowded. In the final Winter there began to appear many artists from the new Komissarzhevsky theatre, a lot of the young, and there came people, altogether unknown to the hosts, and conversations lost their former character. L. D. Zinov'eva-Annibal also that Winter took ill with pneumonia and lay in hospital. The "Wednesdays" could not continue in her absence. But in the Spring, when L. D. returned to the Towers and entirely still weak reclined in an armchair, still a few more times there were Wednesday gatherings. But there was the feeling of an end. And the "Wednesdays" died. And soon also there died their spirit.

"The "Wednesdays" continued for a span of three years. During this time many an event happened. We gathered and conversed during the historical year of 1905. But also in this exceptionally tense revolutionary political atmosphere, when the majority were totally absorbed with politics, at the "Wednesdays" instead there was affirmed and defended the values of spiritual creative life, of poetry, art, philosophy, mysticism, religion. In these discussions we did not feel ourself cut off from life. And in them was a sense of elements unfettering and free. Thereafter ensued an harsh period of Russian life. Much went down further. Everything became differentiated along various currents and spheres of creativity. The level of awareness quite degenerated with the times. The new poetry and the new art became accepted and entered into the general culture. The religio-philosophic trends went deeper. But in the atmosphere, in which the Wednesday discussions occurred, there was something youthful, impelling, inspiring. And the "Wednesdays" always will remain a bright episode of our cultural developement.

Deadening Tradition

(1915 - #192)[1]

I.

Tradition can be alive and active even for our time. But tradition can also be ossified, deadening and moribund. Frequently even the words of a great tradition sound lifeless and dead, evoking nothing, except the memory. A tradition finds justification, as a living, a creative energy. But as a mere remembrance, now already powerless to create life, it cannot make pretense to being a guide for life. And truly there is much in tradition of the ossified and vapid: from dead lips and already repeated dead words. The article of Vyach. Ivanov, "Living Tradition",[2] written in reply to me, has produced upon me the impression of a refurbished stylisation of the old, already moribund Slavophilism. The words no longer sound alive, they are neither energised nor dynamic. V. Ivanov has not succeeded in conveying the feel of a living tradition. He attempts to write in the style of the old Slavophilism. And so deadened already have become so many of the old thoughts and words, that they bestow upon this article by one of the most significant of modern poets, a ponderousness, surmounted only with difficulty. It is difficult to feel, that Slavophilism continues to live in the article of V. Ivanov. This article is striking with its abstractness, it is not connected with the concrete Slavophilism, it repeats the Slavophil ideas, but it nowise conveys the Slavophil feeling for life. And the authentic, the formerly alive Slavophilism was, first of all, a manner of soul, a feeling within life, a tradition familial and of the national way of life, and only thereafter a doctrine and ideology. I tend to think, that Slavophilism played

---

[1] OMERTVEVSHEE PREDANIE. Article originally published 8 April 1915 in newspaper-gazette "Birzhevye vedomosti" (№.14771).
Reprinted since in the sbornik-anthology of N. Berdyaev articles under the title, "Mutnye liki (Tipy religioznoi mysli v Rossii)", Publisher "Kanon+", Moskva, 2004, p. 102-110.

[2] Vide "Bizhevye vedomosti", 18 March.

an enormous role within the history of our national self-awareness, and I believe, that within Slavophilism there was something quite fine, and that from it even still til now have remained vital seeds. Slavophilism was more remarkable of idea than Westernism. But Slavophilism -- was complex a phenomenon, and from it emerged various lines. Certainly even Vl. Solov'ev originates from Slavophilism, and not from Westernism, though he was a fierce critic of a degenerated Slavophilism.

But from Slavophilism has remained also a moribund tradition, dead concepts and words. And from this corpse-like poison we ought to free and cleanse ourself. The living, the creative energy of any current of ideas never degenerates into a mere repeating of the ideas, of the doctrines and teachings of this current. This energy -- is the seed of new life. To continue on with the living, the creative deed of the Slavophils and Dostoevsky -- means to develope and cultivate the seeds cast forth by them, to go not only further than they did, but also to surmount them, sometimes even to scorch them. However, to merely repeat the teachings, the doctrines and the platforms, signifies fidelity to a dead, and not living tradition.

V. Ivanov provides such an abstractly-metaphysical definition of Slavophilism, that amidst it vanish all the sorts of distinctions and oppositions. If the Slavophil -- is everyone, who believes in the mentally-posited and noumenal soul of Russia, then not only am I -- a resolute Slavophil, but the rather that the Slavophil is everyone, who does not recourse to the grounds of positivism and phenomenalism. To admit of the nation as a metaphysical reality, an organism, concealed behind the currents of the phenomena of national life is something possible also for the "Westerniser". The metaphysician and the mystic can also not be a Slavophil. The Russian mystical movement at the beginning of the XIX Century was a matter "Western", and not "Slavophil". And this movement has left behind a legacy within the religious life of the people.[1]

---

[1] Up to the present even among the Russian sectarians, the spiritual Christians, the religious seekers among the people, there tends to be read the "Masonic" mystical literature from the Alexandrian era. [i.e. the period of tsar Alexander I]. I myself have encountered mystics among the people, who have read Mme. Guyon, Boehme etc from books in "Masonic" translations.

THE CRISIS OF ART

On another hand also, V. Ivanov is too keen on wanting to connect his definition of Slavophilism in context with Platonism, with the Platonic world of Ideas.

This however is nowise characteristic of the concrete Slavophilism, which was grounded more within the historical, than the abstract-metaphysical.

The attraction to Platonism -- is moreso the result of contemporary philosophical currents, quite alien to the Slavophils. Quite strong in them was the customary lifestyle, the connection with the historical national flesh. Modern mystical mindsets are totally inapplicable to the Slavophils. The Slavophils -- were not mystics and they did not know the mystics. These were people of a solid earth, the customary lifestyle, attached to everything historically-concrete, with a great deal of sobriety in outlook, and rationality in thinking.

Dostoevsky -- is a man of altogether different a sort, a different type, of different an era. He was already not a Slavophil in the precise meaning of the word, though he also made use of many of the moribund Slavophil concepts. In Slavophilism there was nothing of the catastrophic, there were no apocalyptic outlooks, which are so characteristic of Dostoevsky and Vl. Solov'ev.[1] The since begotten catastrophic sense of life ultimately cuts us off from the Slavophils and makes it impossible to return to their accustomed felicity and their solid footing.

II.

V. Ivanov, in consequence of the Slavophils and Dostoevsky, sees the modern visage of Russia, its mentally-graspable essence, as Holy Rus'. Granted that Russia phenomenal be sinful, but Russia noumenal remains holy, a land of saints, living with the ideals of sanctity. The idea of "Holy Rus'" long since already has lost its freshness and aroma. It becomes all the more and more abstract, bereft of life. The tradition concerning the sanctity of Rus' -- is already a non-living tradition. It is impossible to deny, that in the flourishing of the religious life of the Russian people there have been great saints and ascetics. The image of St. Sergei of Radonezh plays

---

[1] I refer to my book, "A. S. Khomyakov", publisher "Put'".

definitive a role within Russian history. And still not so long ago, already yet still in the XIX Century from the bosom of the religious life of the Russian people there appeared the image of the dazzlingly luminous sanctity of Seraphim of Sarov. The sanctity was fundamental to the spiritual life of the Russian people, just as to every Christian people. Our saints -- are nationally unique, they -- are Russian. But in the sanctity is nothing specifically and exclusively Russian. There were saints in all the Christian lands, and the sanctity represented a flourishing within the life of the Christian peoples. Italy has produced images and visages of sanctity, and it, certainly, has the right to conceive of itself as an "Holy Italy". Sanctity is something at the point of departure, something initially fundamental within the history of the Christian peoples.

The history of the Christian soul has to proceed through asceticism and sanctity. But it is impossible to see in sanctity and the saints the exclusively unique vocation of the Russian people. Holy Rus' authentically exists and has its roots in the life of the people. But not only is Rus' holy, not only in Rus' is there sanctity and the sacred. In sanctity there is nothing exclusively and pre-eminently Russian. A Christian people conceives of its inner intimate visage as sacred at a certain step of its religious developement. But in subsequent centuries the sanctity comes to naught, there are saints all less and less and the ideals of sanctity grow bedimmed. Russia represents no exception to this. Rus' long ago already has ceased to conceive of itself as holy, and this is not a matter of phenomena only, but is in essence noumenal. Holy Rus' was profoundly bound up with the way of life in Rus', as its foundational support. At present words about "Holy Rus'" tend to leave one numb, they do not convey the power of active life. The centre of gravity of the spiritual life has shifted elsewhere.

For V. Ivanov there exists as it were a dilemma: either to believe in "Holy Rus'", as the metaphysical reality of Russia, and to connect in with it the mission of Russia, or to admit of Russia as a metaphenomenon and repudiate its great calling. But no such dilemma actually exists. It is possible to catch sight of a different visage of Russia and differently view its calling. And I no less than V. Ivanov assert, that in Russia one can only believe. And similarly to how the Slavophils believed in Holy Rus', I believe in the *Rus' prophetic*, in the Rus' seeking for the Coming City, the wandering Rus'. Rus' prophetic, searching, and wandering is also the mentally positable secret essence of Russia. Rus' in this is exceptionally unique and dissimilar to any other land in the world. Only in the Russian people is there this searching within everything for the absolute and final, this discontentedness with the relative and mediocre, this prophetic and apocalyptic mindset. And I believe in the prophetic vocation of Russia, in its exceptional destiny to reveal the religiously new within the *finalative* period of world history.

In the exclusiveness of Russia and its mission I believe no less, than the Slavophils, but differently. I have not the possibility to provide the basis and to develop this line of thought within the scope of a small article. I merely render a contrast of one faith by another.[1] I say, moreover, that nationalism to me always appears as something non-Russian, moreso a thing Western, than of Slavophilism. Nationalism places us on a par with all the peoples of Europe and it exists with us, just as there exists with us Capitalism and suchlike phenomena. Contrary to V. Ivanov, I think, that L. Tolstoy -- is Russian deep-down, that within him there was nothing of the Westerniser and that Russia is impossible without L. Tolstoy. The religious and Orthodox searchings of L. Tolstoy, his revolt against world history, his absolute valuations in life, all his fate -- are a great manifestation of the Russian spirit, worldwide in its significance. And the fact of the existence of L. Tolstoy has a greater significance for the fate of Russia, than does its state mightiness. The Tolstoyan repudiation of nationality is more national, than all the national theories. L. Tolstoy did not merely think about Russia, but the rather, was Russia. The noumenal soul of Russia is always sacrificial and renunciatory. The fate in life of Aleksandr Dobroliubov [1876-1945], formerly a decadent poet, and then a wanderer, is moreso indeed characteristic of the inner visage of Russia, than a life Orthodoxly saddled over, and accepting all the Slavophil doctrines and platforms.

III.

The explanations of V. Ivanov concerning the attitude of Slavophilism towards the state authority merely confirm my conviction, that for every Slavophil the state authority is endowed with a transcendent religious sanction. And that what V. Ivanov says about the immanence of the authority within the people, is but a play on words with "immanent"

---

[1] Vide my brochure, "The Soul of Russia" [Dusha Rossii]. Publisher Sytin [1915]. For reading as a public lecture.

and "transcendent". It might be said, that every admitting of the "transcendent" makes it "immanent". But upon these formal grounds we get nowhere. There remains the acute question: does authority possess an origin sacredly-divine or is it naturo-human?

Is it possible to introduce the phenomenon of state authority into the naturo-social developement? The Slavophil view on the nature of authority I regard as at the root of a false absolutisation of the relative, with the extension of absolute categories to the natural-historical process, a consolidation of the spirit of matter. This -- is what is begotten of a religious materialism, confusing and meshing together the absolute and spiritual life with relative and material phenomena. This view leads to a confusing of the Kingdom of God with the kingdom of Caesar, to a rendering unto Caesar that which is of God. Secularisation, which so displeases V. Ivanov and all the Slavophils, is a fulfilling of the words of Christ: "Render unto Caesar what is of Caesar, and unto God that which is of God". Christ made the distinction "of God" and "of Caesar" and He secularised the kingdom of Caesar. The kingdom of Caesar is all this relative, natural, material world, in which reigns the law of necessity, and not the graced freedom of Christ.

Secularisation has as its reverse side the freeing of the spiritual life from the fetters of material necessity. It proclaims the truth and rightful propriety concerning this, that the relative -- is relative, and not absolute, and that what is of Caesar -- is not the Divine. The aspiration towards a secularisation of the state, the family, the economy, science and art is not merely the setting of them loose to freedom, but is also a striving for truth and a repugnance towards falsehood. Truth is the foremost thing of all. And the modern Slavophils tend here to overlook this pathos of the love for truth. They tend not to get choked up over the falsity within the external and visible life. They cling to the conditional life, to words, bereft of content, although totally sincere.

I find it striking, that V. Ivanov considers it possible to repeat the old Slavophil theory, long since toppled by history and having lost all semblance to truth, in regards to this, that in the West the rule of authority was the result from military conquest, but with us in Russia -- it derived in origin purely from the people. The nature of the power of authority in Russia is just as little distinct from the nature of the power of authority in the West, as is the Russian commune distinct from the communes of all lands and peoples. The uniqueness of Russia mustneeds be sought in its spirit, and not in its state and economic forms, which are very uniform everywhere upon the earth. To bestow an inordinate religious significance to trends of state and economic manifestations means to situate oneself in a stage of religious naturalism, of which the Slavophils also were culpable. Secularisation represents a triumph of freedom and truth. The religious illumination of the whole of life ought to come from within, not from the outside. Life has to be inwardly sanctified and illumined, and not merely outwardly sanctified and illumined. And thereof open forth the paths for human activity and human creativity.

It remains completely incomprehensible, why V. Ivanov sees iconoclasm in the call for secularisation. I can assure V. Ivanov, that I am not at all an iconoclast, and in nothing ever have I evidenced a tendency towards iconoclasm. I am an opponent of religious materialism, but I stand resolutely upon the grounds of a religious symbolism. Icons, the cult and all the "flesh" aspects of the religious life posses for me a profound symbolic significance. The secularisation perchance is not directed against the symbolism. It merely represents a liberation from the absolutisation of the materially-relative, from the object-oriented realism within the religious consciousness. All these problems demand indeed a radical reconsidering, it is impossible to resolve them traditionally and simplistically. The whole of the material, object-oriented life -- involves but symbols and signs of the spiritual life and of the spiritual paths of man. But the human spirit can fall into a slavery to a peculiar objectivisation, it can admit of the object-oriented world as the ultimate ontological reality. Then ensues the slavery and decay, and creative life withers. In the old religious consciousness material objects lord it over the human spirit and hinder free movement. Herein is why secularisation is necessary, behind which lies concealed the process of religious developement.

IV.

V. Ivanov makes an attempt to construct a platform and programme from the image of Alyosha Karamazov and he coins a new term, "Alyoshins". But the very great deficiency of the image of Alyosha consists namely in this, that it is so easy to transform him into a platform and programme, whereby for Dostoevsky himself he represented preaching and morals. Alyosha is an exponent for the great searchings of Dostoevsky, but artistically he did not succeed, it is artificial. It is not in Alyosha that there mustneeds be sought the great attainments of Dostoevsky, his genuine insights and revelations. Is it possible to compare Alyosha with the agitated and disconcerting image of Prince Myshkin, -- a genuine revealing of a Christian Dionysianism? Dostoevsky was not given the gift to artistically reflect and religiously preach health. Dostoevsky revealed, that in sickness, and not in health is seen the light, is attained the Divine. "Healthy" is something difficult to conceive of and appreciate with Dostoevsky. He never wrote about the healthy, the clear, the simple, the serenely happy. The Slavophil healthiness and Dostoevsky -- are two different things, with no point of contact betwixt. And I think, that the "Alyoshins" -- are people of spiritual health -- foreign to the "Dostoevschins". Alyosha himself, as a preaching of health, of fullness and a way out from the "Dostoevschins", is not convincing. And they are not the ones intimately close to Dostoevsky, who merely follow his preachings and adopt his platforms and doctrines, just as the Tolstoyans are not intimately close to L. Tolstoy. The tragedy of the individual fate, the sickness of spirit of Raskol'nikov, Stavrogin, Kirillov, Versilov, Ivan Karamazov -- here is where the depths of Dostoevsky is revealed. From Stavrogin it is impossible to construct a programme, and in this is his significance. In the tragedy-novels of Dostoevsky there were prophetic insights, artistic, psychological and religio-metaphysical revelations. Herein is where the genuine Dostoevsky is, and not in the moral preachings and national-church doctrines. The doctrinaire rebirth of Slavophilism preaches a theoretical healthiness, something which preceded the light-bearing sickness of spirit, as experienced and revealed by Dostoevsky. But this healthiness -- is dead, is lifeless. To see the essence of Dostoevsky in Alyosha and "The Diary of a Writer" means to bypass the revolutionary and catastrophic concerns of Dostoevsky. I know, that Dostoevsky wanted to invest much of the new within Alyosha. But in this he did not succeed. Alyosha is lacking in the agitated life. And I have experienced too much in Dostoevsky, merely to become an "Alyoshin". Slavophilism all still remains in the initial healthiness and wholeness, in the natural state of spirit, prior to the catastrophic fragmentation of spirit, prior to the tragedies of Dostoevsky. And the optimism of the modern neo-Slavophils, under the impetus of war, their idyllic view on Russian history and Russian activity disgusts me, as subconscious a lie and an evasion, as an insufficient probing of the tragedies of life both personal and historical, such as have rocked the old idols and shattered the old illusions.

The Charm of the Affectations of Culture

(Vyach. Ivanov)

(1916 - 241)[1]

I.

Vl. Solov'ev said about Nietzsche, that he was not a supra-man, but rather a supra-psychologist. This was wrong. Vl. Solov'ev did not understand Nietzsche and did not esteem him. The tragedy of Nietzsche was a very vital, a very human tragedy. And the whole vital matter with Nietzsche was an expression of the crisis of mankind. And more properly perhaps it is Vyacheslav Ivanov that might be called a supra-psychologist. The giftedness of V. Ivanov is truly amazing and varied. He is, perchance, the most cultured, the most refined and exquisite writer in Russia. A poet and erudite, a mystic and a publicist, a religious philosopher and critic, as well as an artistic man of the world -- he has assimilated and combined all and everything into himself, he wanted nothing and no one to slip by him. But he is first of all and most of all -- a poet, endowed with a rare gift to write verse, but also poetically to transform life. The poetry of V. Ivanov strikes one by its ideational comportment, by its accretive schematic constructs, by its erudition and subtlety, within it are disclosed entire

---

[1] OCHAROVANIE OTRAZHENNYKH KUL'TYR (O Vyach. Ivanove). First published in gazette "Birzhevye vedomosti", 30 Sept. 1916, №. 15833.

Article initially reprinted in 1989 Paris YMCA Press Tom 3 of Berdyaev's writings, -- "Tipy religioznoi mysli v Rossii", p. 516-528.

Reprinted since in the Moscow "Liga" 1994 text, "Philosophiya, tvorchestva, kultury i isskustva", Tom 2, p. 389-399.

Also to be found in the sbornik-anthology of N. Berdyaev articles under the title, "Mutnye liki (Tipy religioznoi mysli v Rossii)", Publisher "Kanon+", Moskva, 2004, p. 111-122.

cultural epochs and strata. This poetry is difficult to read without commentary, in it there is little of the direct or facile, it does not billow about, but instead strikes one by its formal finish and the richness of its content. V. Ivanov of late has managed to reach an even greater levity, which is especially difficult under such a mass of ideational constructs, under such a load from the weight of old cultures. V. Ivanov always shows himself a thinker and it is possible to discern in him interesting mythologems of ideas. But in his religious philosophy he is not original and he is constantly dependent upon various shifting influences. It is quite in character, that V. Ivanov frequently changes his credo -- that he should at one point confess a pagan Dionysianism, then mystical anarchism, and then occultism, then Catholicism, then Orthodoxy and Slavophilism, but inwardly he remains unchanged, in him there is no process occurring and he does not take part in the vital process. He could exist in every time period. He is not at all characteristic of the religio-philosophic searchings nor of the spiritual crisis of our epoch. And he is elusive, he evades all definitions, he wants to be everything. Someone has termed him a courtier. And truly in him there is something in the nature of the courtier. But courtierism is out of fashion. There is no such court in our era, worthy to have so courtly a poet, a refined mage. And he remains a courtier without constant a court, he poetises and billows amidst varied courts. Such people remain little understood for our era, where everything has to be tense, exposed and disjunctive. He wants to live in the charms of the courtly in the utmost meaning of life. In the figure of this poet, somehow considered modernist or even decadent, there is something of the antiquated or even old-fashioned, some sort of fine manners not of our century.

In the figure of V. Ivanov is a refined academism. His erudition is an uniquely aesthetic phenomenon, and this -- is a charmedly-exquisite erudition. Such a refined cultivation exists only with innate philologists. For V. Ivanov it is little to say, that he is philologically very gifted, with him is a philological sense of life, with him is a philological orientation in all spheres, in poetry, in the mystical, in religion, in the political, everywhere. Philology in its utmost sense is art, and not a scientific specialty. And V. Ivanov masters this art to perfection. For him it is possible to say, that to him have been given some sort of altogether unique philosophic revelations about Greece. And he began to live in Greece as a Greek. But is this genuine life? These revelations are not primal revelations and this life is not primal life. V. Ivanov live not in primal being, but in a secondary and philological being, and there everything is revealed to him. He lives in the charmed fascinations of language, the enchantments of words, as a self-sufficient and enclosed modality of being, which does not get disturbed by any of the currents of the primal infinite being, the actual primal-life. V. Ivanov -- is a specialist in tragic Greece, he speaks and writes much about tragedy. In this is shown the defining influence of Nietzsche upon him. But the tragedy of V. Ivanov never leaves behind the vital impression of a dwelled-in experiencing of tragedy, it is instead a second-hand tragedy, reflective being, a philological being. As to philology, I am consistently thinking about not a specialised discipline, but rather a certain principle, which can be rendered both as an universal and an individual element. With V. Ivanov this principle attains the greatest universality and substitutes itself for primal being. The specialty of V. Ivanov -- is Dionysian Greece. He is oriented always towards the archaic and organic epoch. But we ought not to be deceived by mental constructs and slogans. V. Ivanov -- is a typical Alexandrian, in his spirit he is a man of the "Hellenistic" rather than "Hellenic" period, a man of a secondary not primary mode of life, where everything is taken from the derivative reflections of culture and the products of creativity, from philological nuances and subtleties. The Dionysianism of V. Ivanov -- is derivatively-reflective, and not a primary Dionysianism, as it was for Dostoevsky. His intuition of Greece, so striking for everyone, is not a primal ontological intuition, it is an intuition that is secondary and philological, through a complex of culture, art, and language. The antique simplicity has been unapproachable for V. Ivanov. For him philology invariably replaces ontology. For him every tragedy is a tragedy of Aeschylos, and not a tragedy of life. The gods and heroes of Greece always substitute for him in place of the vital reality of our life and life eternal. And for him every Dionysianism is not a phenomenon of life, nor of our eternal life, but rather a phenomenon of Greek culture, Greek religion and mysticism, of Greek literature and art. Known to him are the complicated revelations of culture, but not the simple revelations of being. With this Alexandrianism, with this hyper-philologism of V. Ivanov is connected the complete absence of the psychological, its insufficient interest towards the inner drama of mankind and the creators of culture, towards their vital energy. He prefers ideology over psychology and he is ready to take seriously every ideology and view it as authentic being. Since Dostoevsky is psychologically and in life completely alien to him, ideologically therefore he always loves to connect himself and show interest in Dostoevsky on the secondary-ideological, and not the primary-ontological, not with the wretched of soul. Dostoevsky -- is the antipode to the philologism of V. Ivanov, he is immersed wholly within the revelations of being, and not in the revelations of culture. But suchlike is the nature of pan-philologism, that appropriates everything to itself and encompasses everything with itself. In the lyrics of V. Ivanov there is very little of the psychological, it is saturated by ideology and by the rich materials of the old cultures. For hyper-philologism, for Alexandrianism, for the cultivated academism it is characteristic, that creativity seems not to be accomplished spontaneously, but instead always through the means of the old cultures, of the foreign creativity of former times. Facing the consciousness of V. Ivanov there does not at all stand the acute problem of the relationship of culture and being, of culture and life, he does not sense the tragedy of culture, he is satisfied by culture, enraptured with its riches. In this he is not Russian, he is a Western man, an European, despite his Slavophil ideology.

II.

It is impossible to grasp hold the boundary, separating the mystical constructs of V. Ivanov from the constructs purely philological. He always leaves behind him the possibility of making a retreat, the possibility of not a real, not an ontological understanding of his mystical affirmations. And his mysticism, founded upon the derivative reflection of the genesis of Greek culture, renders itself suddenly and openly receptive to the erudite philologist, to the historian of culture, to suchlike mysticisms which they never took seriously. The erudite philologist and historian of culture is involved in matters derived from mysticism, and he studies it in context of language, in literary relict works, in the cults. V. Ivanov himself -- is an erudite philologist and historian of culture and in his suchlike capacity he is involved in matters from the Dionysian cults of Ancient Greece. And he is moreover -- a remarkable poet, who in his poetry constantly recourses to the erudite marginalia of philosophy and the history of culture. And with him the boundary betwixt primary being and derivative reflected being is obliterated. It is not the word that makes flesh, but rather flesh makes the word, being passes over into word. The word in its essence -- is ontologic. But in the Ivanov world-perception this assuredness vanishes. Nowhere and never is there the sense of the firmness of primal being. In everything -- is a strange instability, the instability of a derivative, philologic state of being. Nowhere is it possible to get down to primary-life, to gauge its authenticity. Amidst this, and it is characteristic of V. Ivanov, that least of all is he a sceptic. He -- is believing, he always affirms, he is filled with the most positive of ideas, he has surmounted everything negative. If it were possible to reduce V. Ivanov to his doubts, to the tormentive polarities in him, then in this it would be possible to get at the primal-life in him. But he always leaves us in that philological state of being, in which everything is overcome and everything is affirmed.

V. Ivanov is not at all a "decadent", he loves to emphasise his overcoming of decadence, his dislike for it. He assiduously sets himself aloof from the French "decadents" and is unjust to them. He -- is not sick, he is completely healthy, in him there is no sort of that exhaustion, there is not the psychologism nor subjectivism of the decadents. His lyrics -- are a cosmic lyrics. But sickness, and decadence -- all are however facts of existence, the crisis of being. For him however everything is derivative and secondary, and therein is where he overcomes all the sickness and crisis. The ease of his overcoming everything negative, the ease of everything positive is explained by this, that it takes place in a secondary, a derivative, a philological mode of being. This philological mode of being however is not non-being, this -- is a certain secondary circle of being, a glittering and magnificent envelope of being. In this splendid sphere is possible a surprising giftedness, enchantment and beauty. In this sphere are possible surprising attainments of artistry, splendid, but not an ontological artistry. And in this sphere the creativity of culture does not reach down to the crisis of culture. This is not that sphere, in which lived the great Russian literature, and in which the great Russian writers lived out their vital drama, it is not the realm of Gogol', of Dostoevsky and Tolstoy, with their enraptured search for ultimate truth. The philological realm -- is an unique realm, living under its own laws.

But nothing in this realm gets down to the primordial depth of being. V. Ivanov -- the most magnificent representative of this realm in Russian literature and culture, produces an impression non-Russian in spirit, his Russianism and Slavophilic ideology leads no one astray. He -- is a Western man thoroughly cultured, filled with a Western quite cultured love for form, the feeling for form and the giftedness in form, a man of cultural conventions. For Russia too mundane, too mundane is his metaphysical essence. His spirit is foreign to the Russian rapturous truth-seeking, the Russian thirst of sacrifice of all the veilings, stripping off every form. The actual teaching of V. Ivanov about a line of descent or down-going, upon which is built his theory of art, -- it would be myopic to confuse this with the Russian sacrificial idea of a down-going. The down-going for V. Ivanov is merely a moment of cultural play-form, cutting short the danger of an ultimate egress beyond the bounds of this world and its forms. Such a gust of ascent and upsurge leads beyond the borders of art and culture, it breaks asunder into another world. V. Ivanov wants however to remain within art and culture, within the beautiful forms of this world, he does not want to permit its despoiling. He invokes and calls for a condescension [sniskhozhdenie], a down-going [niskhozhdenie] to the world and the beauty contained in it. His keen-witted and interesting teaching about a down-going is merely an evidence of his classicism, and this feature likewise is foreign to the Russian spirit. How deeply Russian in comparison with him is that selfsame L. Tolstoy, who in ideological comparison to him seems Western.

III.

V. Ivanov of late loves to insist upon his ontologism. He loves to set forth platforms and at present he preaches an ontologic platform in religious philosophy. But misuse of the words "ontologism" and "ontological" does not mean an already authentic ontologicness. Ontologism for the hyper-philologist is purely an ideological wrapping, a play on words. In the final end, it mustneeds be said, although disliked by V. Ivanov and always subdued in him, psychologism can be a genuine manifestation of life, a condition of being. This mustneeds be said also for individualism, for decadentism, for aestheticism.

Thus the decadentism of Bauldelaire [1821-1867] and the aestheticism of Huysmans [1848-1907] -- are manifestations of life, of a certain existential crisis, and in them there is more of primal-life and primal-being, than in the magnificent and eclectic ontologism of V. Ivanov. V. Ivanov was more authentic, more himself, when he did not misuse the word "ontologism", when he was merely a Symbolist. But his symbolism was scarcely and not so much realistic, even though he termed the symbolic art "*ad realiora*" (i.e. "from the realities to the most real"). In his former years he loved to say, that the important thing was not the "what", but the "how". This was a Dionysian formula. The known condition is important, for example, the ecstatic condition, and unimportant is the ontologic "what". And I tend to think, that for V. Ivanov the "how" is even dearer, than the "what", than the ontologic. He never and in no wise seeks out the ontologic truth. The splendid, the captivating "how" always replaces it for him. It is the magnificent splendour, the eternal "how", and not the eternal "what". The symbolism of V. Ivanov never and nowhere attains ontologism. The ontologism which he now however purports is essentially the contrary and hostile to symbolism, manifest as a form of static dogmatism.

IV.

All these thoughts come to mind, when we read the new book of V. Ivanov, "Furrows and Hedges" ["Борозды и межи", 1916]. Brilliant and interesting, like everything written by him. This anthology of insights from recent years by V. Ivanov is very different from his earlier anthology, "To the Stars" ["По звёздам", 1909]. In that work there was more youthfulness, more daring audacity, rebelliousness, a greater scope and intensity. In the new anthology there is greater tranquility, insight, the sum total of a stormy life, the ultimate introduction of all the elements in classic forms. In its spirit this book is absolutely academic, certainly and refinedly, primly academic, and acceptable as such outside the struggles of the literary and aesthetic parties and currents. Everything in it is in moderation. It is pervaded moreso by a conservative, rather than revolutionary spirit. Apollonism triumphs over Dionysianism.

There are no traces still of the extremes and radicalism of a militant Symbolism. There are sensed preventative measures against youth, against a new danger -- Futurism. There is acknowledgement as well of the mute truth of all the old literary schools. V. Ivanov enters into the role of a teacher, *le maître*. He is foremost a teacher of art, a new sort of academic and a classicist. He renders everything all the more normative. There are no longer appeals to a love of daring, to a Dionysian rapture. He seeks platforms of reconciliation. He is already afraid of the too catastrophically new, whereas formerly he feared it not, he wants to hold on to a certain exquisite cultural middle-ground, to keep it subject to classical norms. He wants also the classicism of a philological, a secondary mode of being. And it is explained, that he was always headed towards this. And it mustneeds decisively be said, that merely our unculturedness, our coarseness and backwardness prevent us ultimately to recognise V. Ivanov and receive him into the bosom of Russian culture, as an incontestable enriching of cultural values, and to the refinement of our cultural life. Amongst the wide circles of the Russian Intelligentsia all which are quite foreign to the refined and elegant forms, connected with former cultural epochs, V. Ivanov would therefore seem a decedent, and to the literary revolutionaries, he would seem representative of some sort of partisan literary party. He -- is a classicist and an academic of new a type, enriching all the valuations of the former decades. And he might struggle against the revolutionary literary tendencies of the latest generation, but he would be moderate at struggle and would appropriate something new into the bosom of his classicism.

V. Ivanov does not sense the crisis of culture, the tragedy of culture, the deep contrary opposition between culture and being. He is satisfied with culture, he wants to remain in it and not make any sort of sacrifices with his culture. Culture represents for him the mystical throughout. He, in following after R. Wagner -- whose influence on him is always felt, believes in the possibility of an universal religious culture. When he speaks about theourgia and invokes theurgy, then with theourgia he conceives everything within the bounds of art, within the bounds of culture, in the enchantment of forms, coming down to this world. But if theurgy be possible, then it should emerge beyond the bounds of culture and art, it presupposes a catastrophic emergence beyond the boundaries of this world. But in V. Ivanov there is not that catastrophic-revolutionary spirit, which Scriabin has.

Scriabin [died 1915] in his rapturously-creative impulse sought not a new art, not a new culture, but rather a new earth and a new heaven. He had a sense of the end of all the old world and he wanted to create a new cosmos. Everything apocalyptic is foreign to V. Ivanov, for he is a classicist as regards his feel for life. Everything that he says about Sobornost' in art, does not signify any sort of world revolutionary turnaround. He believes in the sobornost' of the art and culture of this world, and his faith has as its source not the future, but rather the past -- the sacral culture of Greece. He as it were does not want to admit, that the process of the secularisation of culture is an inevitable process and that it has an hidden religious meaning. This process of secularisation is impossible to halt with a forced-upon norm of Sobornost'. It is impossible to create a religious art, having subordinated it to a theurgic idea. Art needs to be free, it needs to live out its own fate, as also with all culture, it must be but autonomous, religiously immanent, and not forced-upon by a religious norm. To the old sacral organic there is no return. But V. Ivanov does not want to see the meaning of the deeply real processes within being, of all the inevitable differentiations and splinterings. He wants to remain within the enchantments, and his sacral universal art is merely an old enchantment. Hyper-philologism cannot lead it beyond the bounds of the old culture.

V.

The best article of the anthology -- is "Concerning the Limits of Art". In it, V. Ivanov posits an entire theory of art. According to the theory of V. Ivanov, man ascends, but the artist always descends. The artistic form is always the result of a down-going. Ascent of its own accord cannot create art. In the theory of V. Ivanov there is very much that is true. This -- is an excellent phenomenology of artistic creativity. The position of V. Ivanov can be extended even further, it can be expanded to the whole of culture, in all the cultural creativity. All culture is a down-going. And over beyond the creativity of culture is concealed the ascent of man. But in all the spheres of culture there is a cutting-short of this creative ascent and its tendency downwards, its being drawn to this world.

Whether science, or the state, or the management of affairs, or the family, or anything, everything in human culture is a down-going, is an engendering of organic forms through adaption to this world. Science is a down-going of knowledge, the family is a down-going of love, the state is a down-going of human society, etc. The whole teaching of V. Ivanov about down-going is naught else, than that of a strengthening and consolidation forever of the culture of this world, as is the ascent with its beautiful forms. Every objectification is a down-going, a down-going of learning, of the artist, of state activity. In contrast, continuous ascent is a breaking-through beyond the limits of this world, an emergence beyond the bonds of culture, of art and science, of state and family, etc, etc. This -- is an heroic path, a path of audacious sanctity and of audacious genius, and upon this path there is nothing "classical", no sort of classical forms. Onto this path broke through Dostoevsky and Tolstoy, Nietzsche and Ibsen and all those, who were conscious of a world crisis of culture, all those, who thirsted to create a new life, a new mode of being, and not merely new "sciences and arts". These people had presentiment of the end of everything old and the birth of the new. They acutely and painfully sensed the tragedy of creativity: the creative sundering in ascent is always a breaking through to the creation of a new life, a new world. But it is cut-short by the down-going to the old world and it creates merely "sciences and arts", merely state institutions and the forms of the family, mere poems, and philosophic books, and law-imposed reforms. V. Ivanov, remaining within the enchantments of the classical forms of culture, does not know the oppressive and fiery thirst of the quite selfsame man and artist, of his life and creativity. And this is a very Russian thirst. True, V. Ivanov wants a religious culture, religious art. But this yearning of his -- is an archaising yearning, a turning moreso backwards than forwards. And this his thirst for Sobornost' and the sacral proceeds through cultural derivations, through secondary and philological a mode of being. He wishes, that art also in our own time should play suchlike a role, as it did in archaic Greece, but for this he does not venture any sort of sacrifice, -- everything needs instead to flow through the classically beautiful forms. He does not ultimately understand, that within spiritual Sobornost' man goes through the fragmentation of individualism. The archaic, the Greek and medieval Sobornost' are possible as derivations via philology, but no longer still in primal-life, in primal-being.

With V. Ivanov there is no agonised feeling of the onset of a new world epoch, no feeling of the catastrophic. Everything new he would conjoin to his secondary, philologic sort being, and thus would absorb into himself. He would unite and reconcile everything, and he is syncretic in his spirit, he is an altogether unique and refined type of a progressive conservative. But in a fateful manner he remains at the periphery, he does not get through to the core. Everything is at play in him, and he is at play with everything. His playings -- are very refined, very cultured, beautiful and captivating playings. And for Russia it is almost pompous for it to have V. Ivanov, Russians are still too much the peasant for this.

But there is in V. Ivanov something very intimate, hinting at his own primal-life, the very genuine that is in him. I think the gravitating of all his essence, of all his creativity, is towards a religion of feminine divinity. The entire creative visage of V. Ivanov gives basis to suppose, that at the root of his creativity he is immersed in the feminine mystical element, that he also can create only through this feminine principle, through an engrafting of the feminine genius. His very interesting article,

THE CRISIS OF ART

"Concerning the Essence of Tragedy", also speaks on this. His intimate relationship to the feminine -- is not a masculine sort relationship, this is moreso a sense of the feminine in him -- with its especial vagueness, but this all however is with an existential basis. In him the masculine, anthropological principle, the human spirit, is weak. He is rather more astral or aethereal, than spiritual, with everything he is at play with the astral-aethereal glitterings of the outer peripherals. For him the problem of man, man's activity, his masculine creativity is organically foreign. This is too severe, too responsible a problem for him. He penned the beautiful poem, "Man", but this is merely an indicator of his syncreticism, his unusual capacity to absorb everything into himself, to vibrate with everything, in truth to vibrate femininely. But his pathos -- is not an anthropogenic pathos. He is too immersed in the pagan element and the pagan culture, to be anguished by the Christian problem of man. In his attitude towards life, towards Russia, there is something paralytically-pagan. The place of V. Ivanov in Russian culture and art -- is evident and significant, but in the Russian religious movement he cannot hold any especial place.

The Russian Temptation

(As regards "The Silver Dove" of Andrei Bely)

(1910 - 167)[1]

The amazing and unexpected novel of A. Bely, "The Silver Dove" ("Serebryanyi golub'"; 1910), provides occasion anew to consider the age-old Russian theme concerning the relationship of the intelligentsia and the people. But with A. Bely this theme becomes immersed in the mystical element of Russia and is so caught up in this itself, as to be transplanted onto another plane. In the novel of A. Bely there is a scope of genius, an extracted sweep across the people's life, a penetration into the soul of Russia. By virtue of his artistic gift, A. Bely surmounts his subjectivism and penetrates into the objective element of Russia. It decisively mustneeds be said, that the modern Russian art has created nothing more remarkable. In the novel of A. Bely there is sensed a return to the traditions of Russian great literature, but this upon the soil of conquest via the new art. In the "Silver Dove" symbolism is uniquely combined with realism. Bely belongs to the school of Gogol' and genuinely continues on with the Gogol' traditions. The literary-artistic evaluation of the "Silver Dove" is not my task here. Literary critics highly esteem this novel, but they find in it an unevenness, in places a tendency towards caricature, in places a confusion of form, hindering the reader (sometimes in too great an imitation of Gogol'). It can be said, that the image of Katya is altogether unreal, that it has been inserted into the real activity, exactly like a pretty picture. Therefore also the romance of Daryalsky with Katya lacks for life, and the whole of Gugelevo is but an inserted sketch. But it is a place of great

---

[1] RUSSKII SOBLAZN (Po povodu *"Serebryanogo golubya"* A. Belogo). First published in Journal "Russkaya mysl'" nov. 1910, №. 11, p. 104-115.

Article initially reprinted in 1989 Paris YMCA Press Tom 3 of Berdyaev's writings, -- "Tipy religioznoi mysli v Rossii", p. 413-429. The text incorporates some intended 1944 revisions by Berdyaev.

artistic strength. Thus, for example, the place in which there is described, how Daryalsky went astray in the forest along the way from Tselibeev to Gugelevo. How amazing the correlation, of what transpires in the soul of Daryalsky, with that which happens in nature. Daryalsky outwardly has gone astray in the forest, and inwardly his soul has gone astray also. Everywhere with A. Bely the life of nature is conjoined with the life of the soul. Everything in the soul of Daryalsky is going to pieces, but there remains the cosmic aspect of nature and the life of the people. The novel of A. Bely is striking with its artistic truth, with a deep feeling for Russia. There is a profound penetration into the people's life. There is no sort of false idealisation of the people in it. There is no populist saccharine sentimentality. A. Bely has sensed something new in the Russian element, in the Russian people's life, some sort of frightful passion, concealed from the Russian Populist ilk. This frightful passion, this sensuality weighing down upon the spirit, is concealed not only in the Russian mystical sectarianism, but is also in general there within the Russian populist element. The hero indeed of the "Silver Dove" is Russia itself, its mystical element, its nature, its soul. Matrena -- is the Russian earth. The element of Russia is refracted in the soul of the cultural intelligentsia within Daryalsky, but in this it is not an impressionist individualism and subjectivism. The hero -- is not Daryalsky, but instead Russia. Everything, that is sick and impaired within A. Bely, is expressed in Daryalsky, whereas everything in him profound and remarkable, is expressed in his feeling of Russia. With Daryalsky there is a sense of the illusiveness of being. And indeed there cannot but be this illusiveness amidst an attitude of passivity towards being. Only an active attitude towards being provides a sense of the reality of being. The will posits the distinction between the existing and the non-existing. Daryalsky lives expressly under the grip of an obsessive spell, expressively within the atmosphere of a magical enchantment. In the "Silver Dove" there are two sides: the sick and impaired passivity and weakness of Daryalsky and a powerful pervasiveness in the popular element, in the Russian nature. The spirit grasps from this the great, the immensely broad and deep, which is taken up in the "Silver Dove".

The theme of the "Silver Dove" -- is the encounter of the Russian cultural intelligentsia, having lived through all the most recent tendencies from that of Marxism to that of occultism, and subsequently its encounter with a Great-Russian sect of the Doves, in its spirit rather akin to

THE CRISIS OF ART

Khlystyism. A. Bely makes a remarkable inquiry amidst the difficult task of penetrating into the spirit of our mystical sectarianism, and through the sectarianism also into the spirit of the Russian earth in general. The meeting of Daryalsky with the Doves is as it were a meeting of the cultural mysticism with the people's mysticism. The union of Daryalsky with Matrena is also an union of the intelligentsia with the people, from which ought to be born a new Russia. But Daryalsky comes to the people with empty hands, he gives up passively, he brings nothing into the people's life. In regard to the element of the people he is not a light-bearer, not like the sun, not masculine, he does not convey the Logos into the elemental. The ruin of Daryalsky -- is the inevitable result of his passivity, his lack of will. Daryalsky -- is tempted, tempted by Matrena, by the feminine element, by the element of Russia, by the element of the people. There is no trace of the act of will, the act of free choice, of masculine mastery and form, of the masculine Logos within Daryalsky. He lives, as in an enchanted kingdom, he yields passively to the elements, he -- is a medium, through which the magic powers come forth, jostling at him from various sides. Daryalsky is caught up in a nightmarish illusion, here tempting him, there repelling him. The mystical attractions of Daryalsky as one of the cultural intelligentsia, having been a Marxist, and then a decadent, and then somewhat an occultist, these attractions are passive, a medium, without will. The mysticism of Daryalsky is weak and womanish. Opposite him stands the powerful element of the people and draws him towards itself. But the people's mysticism, the mysticism of Kudeyarov and Matrena, is darkly-primitive and elemental, demonic, horrid. This frightsome aspect of the people's mystical element is conveyed by A. Bely quite forcefully. There is a terrible lack of enlightenment in our mystical sectarianism, the absence of the Logos, a dark self-affirmation and plunge into the abyss. A. Bely has sensed this and has conveyed it to us. The "Silver Dove" -- is a gloomy, a distressing book. And within it the people in its mystical element is something mighty, but dark, almost demonically so. The cultural intelligentsia -- lacks will, is sick and passive. A. Bely himself lives under the spell of the Russian element, of Russian fields, of the Russian pockmarked Baba. But no exist is apparent. The novel of A. Bely brings us straight up to the problem of mystical populism.

* * *

Nicholas Berdyaev

The spirit of populism is ineradicably present for a Russian. In no land has there been such a cult of "the people", as there has with us, such an hope to receive truth from "the people", such a thirst to be united with "the people". And nowhere has there been such a splitting away and such fragmentation.[1] Populism has appeared among us in various guises, constantly in metamorphosis: at one point in the form of Slavophilism, then in the form of "Narodnik Populism" in the particular sense of this word, then in the form of Tolstoyanism, it has crept even into Russian Marxism, and now it assumes a form clearly mystical. Mystical populism -- is a most profound aspiration of the Russian national spirit. Mystical populism is deeply lodged within the nature of the Russian will, and perhaps also in the Russian lack of will. Behind the Russian populism even in the positivist form there lies hidden a peculiar mysticism, a subconscious mysticism. Nowadays mysticism has become fashionable, and therefore also populism has taken on a mystical hue. The intelligentsia of the new mystical type go to the people not for true revolutionism, but for true mysticism. They hope to receive from the people not social truth, but rather a religious light. Yet the psychological attitude towards the people remains such as it was earlier: this thirst to yield itself up to the people and from it to receive light, this indeed worship towards the people, this incapacity for a masculine solar radiance, for a mastery of the elements, for a bearing of meaning into it. The Russian intelligentsia in essence always was feminine: capable of heroic exploits, of sacrifices, of giving up its life, but incapable of masculine activity, it never possessed an inner foothold of support, it yielded itself up to the elements, it was not a bearer of the Logos. This is perhaps connected with the fact that in Russian history there was never a chivalrous knighthood. There are features of semblance, innate to the Russian revolutionary and the narodnik-populist of the old form, and to the Russian decadent and mystic of the new form. Both the one and the other is under the grip of the feminine element of the people and is powerless to convey into it the formative principle of the Logos; both the one and the other is prepared to worship the people, one in the name of a revolutionary light, the other in the name of a mystical light; both the one and the other nonetheless remain alienated from the people, from the sweat of the

---

[1] [1944 revision]: All this has been halted by the Russian Communist Revolution.

THE CRISIS OF ART

organism of the people, and they go to the people with empty hands, and in the element of the people they desire to receive that, which they cannot receive first-hand, from whence and from whither the people itself derives its light. The most remarkable Russian writers wanted to believe in that, in which the people believes, and to believe suchlike thus, as the people believes.. In the name of this they consented to make themself simplistic. And they failed to note, that in this was a terrible lie and false from the point of view of the people's faith itself. The people believe that in faith they see the true light. The faith itself and the truth revealed within it stands higher than oneself. Yet from the perspective of Russian mystical populism, the people would be higher than faith and truth, and that whatever would be true, in whatever the people believes. Both the Slavophils, and Dostoevsky, and many others also were not fully free of this false worship towards the people and its faith. This worship towards the national element was expressed both in our Old Believer ritualism, and it was expressed also in the nationalisation of the Orthodox Church, which has weakened in us the sense of universality. And upon this rests also all the Tolstoyanism, so very in character for Russians. In another form these national peculiarities are expressed also in the camp of the atheist-populists, and therein too they have sought for truth from the people and the people they have posited as higher than truth. Populism -- is a chronic Russian ailment, impeding the creative renaissance of Russia. Populism, beaten and banished in one form, swiftly is reborn in another. The final form of populism -- is a mystical populism. Mystical populism is a lie and temptation from the religious point of view and a dangerous hindrance from the cultural and societal point of view. The alternate historical task for the Russian self-consciousness would be to defeat all the forms of the temptation of populism, i.e. radically to alter our attitude to the people's element. Amidst this, the social truth of populism would still remain. The new national self-consciousness, full of messianic hopes, would become masculinely-active, sun-like, light-bearing, a bearer of the Logos, providing form and mastery over the elements. But this masculine principle of the Logos is preserved within the Church, it is not there in the sectarianism, which as such is always elementally-feminine. In the non-church mystical populism there is no Logos, there is a false semblance of the feminine, a passive yielding of itself to the elements. The Church only is masculine and only within the churchly consciousness is there an active attitude towards the elemental, i.e. a requisite correlation of the masculine and the feminine. Both the non-religious Russian populists, and the non-churchly Russian mystics are ready always to surrender themself to the power of the element of the people, amidst a lack of ability to bring anything into it.

The thirst for dissolution, for yielding -- is purely a Russian thirst. The visage of the pockmarked Baba Matrena eternally tempts, it pulls into the pagan national element. This inclination to the apotheosis of the Russian national element is there also in the Russian mystical sectarianism, in Khlystyism, it is there in the Old Believer ritualism, it is there also in historical Orthodoxy, insofar as within it the Church was too nationalised and weakened in its universality. Russia is eternally threatened by the danger of a pagan-elemental nationalism, reactionary both in the religious attitude, and in the socio-cultural. This reactionary element was expressed even in the Russian Revolution.[1] And in Russian mysticism there is always sensed this inclination. Only the universal Logos can be set in opposition to every elemental reactionism and revolutionism, only the truth of the universal Church can be set in opposition to all the forms of our reactionary and revolutionary paganism, to the reactionary and revolutionary feminine mysticism. That Russian element, which is to be sensed in the visage of Matrena, is not annihilated by the universal Logos, but only enlightened, and given form. Matrena awaits a man and for too long a time does not find him. Indeed both our elemental Black Hundreds movement is tempted by the visage of Matrena, just as also by it can be tempted our [Red Hundreds] revolutionary movement. But the danger of primitive-pagan reaction is both there and here, since the reaction is everywhere there where is not the Logos, not masculinity, not the solar, conveying meaning. Matrena, this artfully-ingenious symbol of the Russian people's element, ought not to tempt and cripple, and the masculine ought to master it. Only then will universal truth defeat our reactionism and revolutionism.

A. Bely ties in the mystical sect of the Doves, akin in spirit to Khlystyism, with revolution. He brings the mystical element nigh close to the revolutionary element. But Russian Khlystyism is sooner reactionary, than revolutionary. Khlystyism is a reaction of the pagan popular element against the Logos. Khlystyism is revolutionary in regard to the Church,

---

[1] [1944 revision]: This was written after the first, the lesser Russian Revolution [of 1905]. But partially this can be said also about the second, the major Russian Revolution [of 1917].

namely because it is reactionary. Reactionary is everything, that rises up against the churchly Logos, against universal Meaning in the name rather of a primordial element, -- of an element, preceeding any light of consciousness, any self-consciousness of the person. Kudeyarov -- the head of the Doves -- is a quite deep, mystical reactionary, and in him -- is the elemental, hostile to the Logos, hostile to the mastering of the land. In Kudeyarov there is no relationship to the Countenance of Christ, there is not that self-consciousness of the person, of that which is its affirmation within God, which also only can be connected with Christ. In sectarianism there is not the Face of Christ and there is not the person, there is only the Spirit -- the Spirit within man. And the kingdom of Spirit here is an impersonal kingdom, prior to Christ, less, and not moreso, than Christianity. Kudeyarov and Matrena -- are not a mystical Christianity, but rather a mystical paganism, primitively prior to Christ, prior to the Logos, prior to the person. The elemental mystical sectarianism is reactionary also in regard to culture, since culture is inseparably connected with the universal Logos, with the victory of the light-bearing masculine over the elemental feminine. Everything genuinely progressive and liberating is connected with the mysticism of the Logos, and not with the mysticism of the elemental. The Logos however abides within the Church. The pitfall of any sectarianism, and of the mystical Russian sectarianism, -- the pitfall of any reactionism -- is in a splintering-away from the Church, into rather self-affirmation. A false relationship to the Church and to the universal churchly consciousness engenders all the inclinations of sectarianism. And Khlystyism is culpable first of all in its falling-away from the Church, in its self-affirmation against the Universal Church. And from whence thus derives the domination of the pagan element upon the Khlysty, with the force of nature, accepted as grace, and from whence also is the demonism.

  A. Bely penetrates deeply into the mystical element of the people. But he overlooked that side of popular life, which for the Russian people is connected with the Church. There is much paganism also in the Orthodox churchly way of life, much of that, which A. Bely described in the traditional-mould type of the priest Vakula. But there is also a genuine aspect to the universal truth of the Church of Christ. There is a nook in the soul of the Russian people, in which lives the genuine churchly Christian truth, -- an enlightened corner. A. Bely does not sense this, and with this A. Bely connects nothing. And indeed only the churchly mysticism is enlightened and connected with worldwide culture. There is no solarity nor masculinity in the mysticism outside the Church, however much enticing or frightful. If there were no corner in the soul of the Russian people, by which the churchly Logos should prevail, then there would be no sort of hope of a great world future facing the Russian people. It is impossible indeed to connect this future wither with Kudeyarov, or with Daryalsky, for in them is darkness and passivity. A. Bely has disclosed this with the power of an artistic intuition. A. Bely artistically senses the lie within mystical populism, although he himself is not fully free of it. He exposes the darkness of the people's mysticism outside the Church and also the lack of will in the cultural mysticism. Reading the "Silver Dove", one comes more strongly to the awareness, that it is impossible to rely upon either the people, or upon the intelligentsia, or upon the civil powers, or upon the clergy, or upon whatever the human and natural element, but instead one ought to rely upon the Church as an organism of mystical universality. The light of churchly consciousness and the power of the churchly will ought also to carry over into the life of the people, and into the life of the intelligentsia. The idolisation of the people, just like the idol-worship of any natural element, is a lie and a sin. Worship is proper only to God, and submission only to His Church.

In the elemental sort mysticism the person is neither discovered nor affirmed. Person as such is formed and comes to an unshakable self-consciousness only within the Church of Christ. Elemental mysticism is immersed all completely within nature, it does not emerge from the cycle of nature. Person however can be affirmed only in the surmounting of nature, within the order of freedom. The Khlysty vigils wholly still dwell immanently in nature, in them is no transcendence into the graced order of freedom. And therefore person amongst the Khlysty becomes lost. Person does not exist in the mystical ecstasy of the Doves, as described so remarkably by A. Bely. The person as such does not exist among them, nor does freedom. With both the Khlysty and the Doves the awaiting the descent of the Holy Spirit is in essence a naturalistic pantheism, in which always drowns both the person and freedom. And again the Logos fails to enlighten nature, again there is not disclosed a transcending egress from nature, there is still neither the person nor freedom. The gravitation of the cultured and the semi-cultured strata to the Khlysty and to mystical popular sectarianism is an indicator of a crippling, of a feminine pliancy, of a fading out of the person and of freedom. Within our mystical sectarianism is hidden an enormous mystical thirst and mystical energy. But one

THE CRISIS OF ART

perishes, in femininely surrendering it away. This energy mustneeds be masculine, actively mastered, this thirst mustneeds be satisfied by an utmost meaning. And only the churchly universal Logos gives possibility to manfully master the mystical energy and actively to satisfy the mystical thirst. A false correlative identification of the masculine and the feminine -- is a great sin and a terrible pitfall. We too are sinners in this, and the ground under us is breaking apart. The ruination of Daryalsky is deeply symbolic. This ruination is not only from a false attitude of cultural mysticism to the people's mysticism. Such ruination exists also with the Russian revolutionary-intelligentsia in their false relationship to the element of the people. Our cultural intelligentsia society comes to ruin through a crippling, from its absence of manfulness, from its sundering from the Logos, from the fading off of the universal meaning of life. Even in a moreso masculine and active surrender to Matrena, to the element of the people, they still nonetheless deify the people, whilst having lost God; the moreso feminine and passive are ultimately enticed to Matrena, and with longing they are drawn to the mystical element and perish. Such a mystical populism -- is a terrible lie and a terrible temptation. The falsehood and danger lie hidden in the very settings of the problem of the intelligentsia and the people, of culture and the primitive element. It possesses a religious meaning only in the correlation of the masculine and the feminine, of the Logos and the earthly element. With the Church there is not only the masculine Logos, but also there is eternal femininity; through the Virgin Mary the Logos has come into the world, and to the true masculinity this cult of eternal femininity is innate, which is contrary to a false power of femininity. Only the churchly consciousness settles the false problem and resolves the problem with the true. A. Bely with genius senses the elemental in Russia, of the Russian people, of Russian nature, of Russian fields and hollows, the Russian Baba. This -- is the feminine earthly element. But he does not know the Logos within the Russian national consciousness and therefore he does not sense the masculinity of our worldwide mission. Only within the Church obtains the masculine principle of the Logos, and it is the churchly side of our national life that A. Bely has overlooked.

*   *   *

Nicholas Berdyaev

A. Bely himself lacks the ability to master the mystical element of Russia by the masculine principle of the Logos, he is in the grip of the feminine element of the people, he is tempted by it and he surrenders himself to it. This is sensed within all his creativity, everywhere in it is the pursuit of his feeling of an illusory being, in a nightmarish bewitchment, of which his work is full. The mysticism, reflected in the creativity of A. Bely, -- is predominantly feminine, frequently becoming transformed into a mere medium. A. Bely -- is an elemental populist, an elemental nationalist, eternally tempted by Matrena, by the fields, the hollows and the inns, eternally thirsting to become dissolved away into the Russian element. But the less there is in him of the Logos, of the masculine churchly consciousness, the moreso he wants to replace the Logos by surrogates -- by critical gnosseology, by Rickert, by the methodologies of Western culture. There it is that he seeks for manly discipline, for providing form to the chaos of the Russian mystical element, for the averting of disintegration and pitfalls. The more he is tempted by Matrena, the more he is drawn towards dissolution in the mystical element of Russia with its frightful and dark chaos, and all the more he comes to worship gnosseology, methodology, scientificity, criticism etc. The cult of Matrena and the cult of methodology -- are two sides of one and the same splitting asunder, of dissociation of the earth and the Logos, of the primitive elemental and of consciousness. In the critical methodology and gnosseology there is thus as little of the Logos, as also there is in Matrena and Kudeyarov. And certainly not in such methodology, as might be mastered by Matrena. The blustering, chaotic, dark element of the people can be mastered only by the churchly masculine Logos, and not by methods, not by gnosseology, not by Rickertism. The Russian land, filled with mystical a thirst, is drawn to the churchly great Reason, and not to the small gnosseological reason. In critical methodology there is so little of the Reason-Logos, as also there is in the mystical sectarianism, and there lacks a masculine will in both the one and the other.[1]

Simultaneously with the "Silver Dove" there has come out also another remarkable book by A. Bely, "Symbolism" [1910]. And in it with a striking degree of talent is disclosed another side of A. Bely, a side not

---

[1] Since the time, when this was written, A. Bely has sought salvation from the Russian mystical pathos not in Rickert and the Kantian methodology, but in Steiner and the anthroposophic methodology.

apparent in his poetry, in his compositions, nor in the "Silver Dove". This side of A. Bely -- is philosophical, gnosseological, methodological, differentiating, cultural. The verses of Bely -- are purely Russian, national, populist, Eastern, a feminine element, passive, enveloped by nightmares and presentiments, nigh close to the irrational. The Russian fields and the pockmarked Babas, the hollows and the taverns -- are intimate and inborn to *this* A. Bely. In A. Bely there is much of a mystical Slavophilism, -- a Slavophilism disturbed and in tumult, catastrophic, connected with Gogol' and Dostoevsky (but not with Khomyakov, in whom the masculine Logos was too strong). A. Bely, as a philosopher -- is quite purely a Westerner and cultured. He does not love Russian philosophy, the Slavophil consciousness is foreign to him, his consciousness is exclusively Western. To *this* A. Bely Rickert is closer than Vl. Solov'ev, Nietzsche is closer than Dostoevsky, Jakob Boehme is closer than St. Seraphim, differentiated methodological philosophy is closer than synthetic religious philosophy. With a methodological strictness, he is almost scientifically prepared to engraft onto the Russian the Western mysticism of Eckhardt and Boehme, so dissimilar to Kudeyarov and the Doves. But thus what transpires with the contradictions of the Eastern-Russian elemental mysticism of A. Bely and his West-Europan cognitive philosophy? In the elemental mysticism of A. Bely there is sensed the nightmarishness and illusoriness of being. The nightmarishness and illusoriness of being remains also in his philosophic consciousness. In the "Symbolism" tome there is an amazing, in places an ingenious chapter entitled, "The Emblematics of Meaning", in which A. Bely develops an unique philosophic system, nigh close to Fichteanism, but moreso artistic, than scientific. In this peculiar Fichteanism there is sensed the splitting-asunder from being and a fear of being. A. Bely makes divine only the creative act proper. God does not exist, as the Existent, but the creative act is made divine, and hence God is created, He is a creative value, a requirement, but is not being. And in the process of creativity there is no end, no completion within absolute being. The creative process transpires under the nightmarish grip of a bad infinity, an ugly multiplicity. With A. Bely and innate to him in spirit is that the Son is born without the Father, the Logos has no paternity, and therefore the word is human, and not of God. And man possesses no origin of descent. A. Bely climbs upwards along the steps and he destroys each step, he hangs suspended over the empty abyss, and never and nowhere does he get with this nightmarish climb upwards, since there is no end-point, there is no that

One to Whom he goes, there is only the eternal ascent upwards, the eternal dawn, the endless creativity from nothing and for nothing. This -- is a philosophy of illusionism, of the apparition, of the beauty of the nightmare. Even Rickert -- is but a rung, upon which A. Bely attempted so assiduously to stand, -- and with ingratitude he demolishes it and sneers over it wittily and brilliantly. There remains only the pure creative act, but without a bearer, without a substrate, without an existent. A. Bely dwells in this truly terrible delusion, that there might be *an approach* to the Absolute, to true being, to freedom. But from the Absolute, from true being, from freedom there is possible only an exit. Towards the Absolute there are no paths, which should start separate from the Absolute, on the first rung one mustneeds already be with God, in order to hoist oneself up upon the following rungs, and it is impossible to have cognition without an initial connection with the Absolute, without the presence of the Logos in cognition. It is impossible to approach nigh to God without the help of God, it is impossible to know truth without the Logos, begotten of the Father, it is impossible to reach the Absolute, exiting the relative. There are no pathways towards being, laying across the empty abysses, one mustneeds initially dwell within being, in order to move within it. Being within God and with God is not an end of dynamic motion, but only the beginning of true movement. Synthetic integral wholeness ought to be present also at the beginning, at the first rung, and not only at the end, at the summit, since without synthetic integral wholeness it is impossible to take a step, it is impossible to move, and equilibrium is lost. God -- is real, and not a mere imperative, His being does not depend upon our creative act. But on our creative act the world is dependent, we participate in the enlightenment and transfiguration of the world, in reunion with the Creator.

      A. Bely in his philosophic consciousness thus is cut off from the Logos, just as also he is in his mysticism. And in both the one and the other -- is an illusoriness of being, an hybrid of value with a nightmare, without any ontological foundations. In this is rooted also the gravitation of A. Bely towards the Western occult discipline, slipping itself into his writings. A. Bely searches for discipline, consciousness, formation -- entirely from without, instead of gaining all this from within. It is impossible to receive discipline of will or discipline of consciousness externally from the methods of critical philosophy or the methods of occultism, it is possible to be discovered only within the depths of one's own spirit, in union with the churchly Logos. In A. Bely I see a false combination of Slavophilism and Westernism, a false connection of East and West. But he posits this problem with an especial acuteness and anguish. A. Bely is too much the Slavophil and too much the Westerniser. He is attracted to the Eastern mystical element, and to the unutterable mysticism of the Western form. But the unutterable Western mysticism denies this fundamental religious truth, that mysticism is expressed in the Logos-Word. Mysticism inexpressible in the Word is anti-church and anti-religious. As an artist, A. Bely surmounts individualism and subjectivism, but only as an artist. As a philosopher, A. Bely remains cut off from the Logos. This state of being torn asunder plunges him into an inescapable pessimism. The creativity of A. Bely is trapped within that selfsame inescapability, as is also the creativity of Gogol'. A. Bely does not believe, that it is possible to discover the light of the Logos within the depths of the spirit, in vain he seeks the light, at one point in the Eastern element of the people, and at another point in the Western consciousness. He lives in the dense and strained atmosphere of the Apocalypse, his experience is apocalyptic-catastrophic. And in this is all his significance. In him everything is taken to the limit, everything gravitates towards the end. But in A. Bely there is sensed also an apocalyptic femininity, a peculiar mystical receptiveness, and through it come forth the apocalyptic bursts. Together with this, in A. Bely is sensed an ethical and right-loving nature. And eternally it threatens him with a sharing in the fate of Gogol'.

When one penetrates into the mysticism of our days, one senses especially the truth, taught by the Eastern Christian mystics, the truth about the great significance of a mystical sobriety. Mystical sobriety reflects also a manliness of spirit, the constant opposition to any sort of a medium, to any sort of a crippling complacency of the feminine element. The greatest model of mystical manliness is given us in the image of St. Seraphim of Sarov. In Khlystyism there is not this manliness, there is no sort of manliness. Nor is there this manliness in the contemporary cultural mysticism. The manliness of St. Seraphim ought to be carried over into the element of the people.

*   *   *

Nicholas Berdyaev

The "Silver Dove" -- is the first part of a trilogy, which is named "East and West". The "Silver Dove" posits anew the age-old problem of East and West. I do not know, how much farther along that A. Bely is with his goals, but the first part of the trilogy has shown a tremendous giftedness in what has come out in the series already. One senses a great discord between the verses and the consciousness of A. Bely, but this is the right of an artist, who transcends all the discord. Of such a prerogative is the "Silver Dove". A. Bely has detected much that is new in Russia, much that was not yet evident even in the greatest Russian writers. The problem of East and West -- is purely a Russian problem. Russia stands at the centre of East and West, it is bound up with world history, and within it only can there be synthetically decided the age-old dispute. Not in vain was all the Russian self-consciousness of the XIX Century filled with the disputes of Slavophilism and Westernism. This dispute appears in all ever anew forms. And there will come a time, when we ought ultimately to surmount both Slavophilism and Westernism. There is a provincialism both in the one and the other current, there is not an authentic universalism in either the one or the other. Within the national flesh and blood there ought to be affirmed the universal reason, the truth of all humanity. Our national-religious vocation can only be conceived of as the vocation of intermediary between East and West, an uniter of the truth of the East with the truth of the West, the transformer of the two types of Christian religious experience and the two types of culture within the life of a single humanity. Our national religious mission therefore is contrary to any sort of reactionary nationalism. The new creative self-consciousness cannot be either entirely of Slavophilism, nor of Westernism, it is not the slave of either the Eastern primitive element, nor of the Western mindset. The surmounting of Slavophilism and Westernism will also be an indicator of our national maturity, of national self-consciousness. Slavophilism and Westernism -- are the things of a youthful immaturity, the travails of the birth of self-consciousness. The historical tasks of Russia now in all spheres ought to be a mature and manly national self-consciousness, bound up with the universal religious consciousness. Into this national self-consciousness would enter in all the Slavophil truth and all the Westerniser truth, and there would be overcome the false provincialism of the Slavophil and the Westerniser. Westernism indeed also is provincialism. In the West there are no Westernisers, the Westernisers -- are a provincial Russian phenomenon. The worship of the Western European mentality, of Western

THE CRISIS OF ART

European science and culture, is an idolatry. Consciousness can only be universal, and not Western European; science and culture cannot be exclusively the attainment of a Western European provincialism.

Praise befits the artist, who has drawn us anew to the problem of East and West, and who restores our literature from the minor to the great. To A. Bely belongs a foremost place amongst our artists. His theme is infinitely profound and important, quite serious and shaking. Within A. Bely himself everything is symbolic, everything expresses unrest. In him becomes expressed more strongly and more extremely that which exists in many of the "Russian lads". His giftedness is so great, that the fear for him transforms itself into a fear for many Russians. But let there descend upon him and upon all the "Russian boys" the graced power of the masculine Logos.[1]

---

[1] [1944 revision]: The masculine Russian power has awakened in Soviet Russia after the Revolution. But its awakening was sundered off from the Russian spiritual elements, and with this fracture was connected much of the bad. Such is the Russian fate.

Murky Visages

(1923 - #60,3)[1]

The unfinished reminiscences of Andrei Bely concerning A. Blok read with a gripping interest. Though at the centre of these reminiscences stands the figure of A. Blok, they are immeasurably broader in their scope. And the theme of these reminiscences is very profound. This -- is a theme about far-sightedness, things beheld at the beginning of the century by the souls of the poets, alert to the coming, and prophetic in disposition. And it is possible still further to delineate this theme: the revelation concerning the Sophia of Vl. Solov'ev, of A. Blok and A. Bely, and the relationship of these revelations to the presentiments of the coming revolution. But is the Russian Revolution an authentic revelation of Sophia within Russian life? Herein it becomes necessary to radically expose a growing lie, connected with a tempting confusion, the mixing up of an expected revelation of spirit, of a revolution of spirit, with the Russian external Revolution of 1917. A. Bely[2] -- is the greatest Russian writer of the last decade, unique

---

[1] MUTNYE LIKI (A. Bely. *Vospominaniya o A. A. Bloke*). First published in the Berdyaev-edited sbornik-anthology, "SOPHIA: Problemy dukhovnoi kul'tury i religioznoi philosophii" ("SOPHIA: Problems of Spiritual Culture and Religious Philosophy") -- Berlin, Obelisk, 1923 (Kl. № 60,3), p. 155-160, as the third of three articles contributed by Berdyaev to this sbornik.

(The other two articles are: "The End of the Renaissance" (written 1919 in Moscow; first published as booklet in Peterburg, publisher Epoch, 1922 (Kl. № 17|60,1) p.21-46); and also "The 'Living Church' and the Religious Rebirth of Russia" (Kl. № 60,2), 125-134.)

Our present article was republished in the 1993 tome of Berdyaev articles under cover title "*Mutnye liki*" ["*Murky Visages*"], taking its name from title of Berdyaev's article of same name contained therein. Moskva, 2004, Kanon+, p. 324-334.

[2] *trans. note*: pseudonym of Boris Nikolaevich Bugaev, 1880-1934.

with genuine glints of genius. And A. Blok [Aleksandr, 1880-1921] -- is actually the most remarkable Russian poet after Fet [Afanasy, 1820-1892]. A. Bely as an event is larger and more significant than Blok, but Blok is more the poet. And here they both in the year after the Revolution are in the grip of the tempting lie, captivated by fraudulent figures, and unable to discern spirits. Both became obsessed with the elements of the Revolution and failed to find in themself the powers spiritually to rise above it and surmount it.

The prophetic character of Russian literature is amazing. Over the course of all the XIX Century it was full of forebodings of the coming revolution, it was extraordinarily alert to the underground rumblings. Pushkin even was agitated by the possibility of revolution in Russia, and he foresaw its character. Lermontov writes in a jolting verse: "There will come a year, for Russia a black year, when the tsar's crown will fall".[1] Tiutchev was all the time distressed over the problem of world revolution. Konstantin Leont'ev, during the decade of the 80's, in an era seemingly auspicious for the Russian monarchy, predicts, that Russia would infect Europe with Communism and it would result in Europe infecting China with Communism. And finally there appears Dostoevsky as an authentic prophet of the Russian Revolution, and to the very depths he exposes its spiritual foundations and gives it an image. Dostoevsky ultimately became conscious of what was transpiring with the revolutionary spirit, he revealed its inner dialectic and foresaw its inevitable consequences. The revolution of the spirit began first of all in Dostoevsky, with him began the new epoch, as it were a new world aeon. Even Vl. Solov'ev in this regard is not so characteristic. For A. Bely and A. Blok, Vl. Solov'ev is merely a front for the expression of their own sophianic experiences and presentiments. In the actual and total assimilation of Vl. Solov'ev they are both very distant, and he would not have recognised them. What has A. Blok in common with Vl. Solov'ev as a philosopher, as a Catholic or Orthodox, with strivings towards an unification of the Churches? Vl. Solov'ev believed first of all in Christ, and moreover in Sophia; A. Blok believed first of all or wanted to believe in Sophia, whereas in Christ he never did believe. What in common do the optimists of the coming future, A. Bely and A. Blok, have with the remarkable work of the prophetic spirit of Vl. Solov'ev -- in the "Tale about the Anti-Christ"? In this turning towards what is to come, to the coming

---

[1] *trans. note*: from 1830 poem " Predskazanie" ("A Prediction").

catastrophe, Vl. Solov'ev, as an apocalyptic pessimist, exposes that Anti-Christ spirit, which so captivates A. Blok and A. Bely. Only a few sophianic verses of Vl. Solov'ev correlate with those of A. Blok. Vl. Solov'ev is very interesting as regards his themes, but is all the same a second-rate poet, and much gets lost along the way in the poetry of A. Blok, and it is impossible that he can be a Solov'evite, as only several of his verses would even suggest it. There is only one thing in Vl. Solov'ev that A. Blok and A. Bely have heard:

> The Eternal Feminine now
> In body incorrupt to earth is come.
> In the light unfading of the new goddess
> The heavens merge with the watery deeps.[1]

And here arises the question about the significance and meaning of the sophianic dispositions in the Russian mystic, of Russian religio-philosophic thought, of Russian poetry. The sophianism of Vl. Solov'ev indeed has influence not only on A. Blok and A. Bely, but likewise upon Florensky, Bulgakov, Ern. The cult of Sophia is very characteristic of the Russian spiritual currents. And it is remarkable, that the sophianic attitude towards Russia and the Russian people assumes two polar opposite tendencies: the one sees the sophianic aspect in the Russian autocratic monarchy, while the other sees it in the Russian Revolution. In both the one and the other instance there is made a god of the wise feminine element of the people, be it white or red, the white waits for the elemental feminine principle within the life of the people, and not for the masculine spirit, not from the spiritual activity of man. With Vl. Solov'ev himself there was not this making a god of the people's primitiveness, he was never a mystical populist. But his intimate cult of Sophia is prepared to use him for the basis of a mystical populism.

In the teachings of Vl. Solov'ev about Sophia and in his mystical poetry there was promulgated a sort of lie, which tended to engender the murkiness in our spiritual currents. Vl. Solov'ev mixed up and confused Sophia, the Wisdom of God, the Heavenly Virgin, with an earthly goddess, with an earthly femininity. And therefore there became possible the acute sentiments over Sophia Petrovna, Vl. Solov'ev's object of love, in whom

---

[1] *trans. note*: cf. Vl. Solov'ev's 1898 poem "Das Ewig-Weibliche".

with the Third Testament -- Sophia becomes combined with the Second Testament -- of Peter. And therefore only possible became the notes under the inscription "Sophie". And therefore so tormentive for Vl. Solov'ev was the meeting with Anna Schmidt, an image of femininity of the greatest genius, the likes of only whom he was to know in his entire life, and yet so unattractive, so repelling for him. Sophia was seductive and alluring for Vl. Solov'ev, in his romantic languor and swooning, an eternal thirst for meetings and encounters with the Unknown, and an eternal enchantment, an eternal possibility of confusion and substitution. Sophia for Vl. Solov'ev was not the Virgin of his soul, his virginity, of his purity and chastity, as it was in the teachings of Jacob Boehme, a verymost profound and pure teaching concerning Sophia. The Sophia of Vl. Solov'ev was not the Virgin, which man had lost and which he again has to find as his *Virginitat*, his virginalness; this -- is the femininity, in which the heavens get too confused with the watery deeps, with the earthly element. And this cult of Sophia does not strengthen, but rather weakens man, it does not restore the integral wholeness of his androgynic image, but rather separates its apart. Such a Sophia therefore can appear in whatever the guise pleases it, it can be rendered not only as Heavenly Virgin, but also as the earthly dissolute feminine, it can turn out either as "reactionary" or "revolutionary" an element of the Russian land. And upon this soil there are cultivated irrational mystical currents, hostile to the Logos, the Word. And striking indeed is this passivity of the Russian religious mystical searchings. Russians await a new Revelation, a revelation of the Spirit, of Sophia, they sense themselves pervaded by mystical currents, they surrender themselves to the callings of an unknown and mysterious what is to come, they bow before the mystique of the element of the Russian people, of the Russian earth. This is difficult for the Western peoples to comprehend. Western peoples tend to set themselves an active task and they make the spiritual efforts to accomplish it. Their mysticism teaches them with ways of spiritual ascent. Their theosophy teaches them to develop new organs of perceptivity. And least of all do they understand a condition of expectation, of a passive mystical trembling in facing what is to come. They either make a revolution, or they struggle against it, but they do not give in passively to its undiscerned mystical meaning. Russian boys however, those of a mystical disposition, await a revelation of what is to come, they strain their sight towards new horizons, they sense themselves wrapped up in a mystical element, the meaning of which remains for them incomprehensible and inexpressible. A. Blok most of all is obtrusive with his "inarticulateness", his "gut-feeling", his incapacity in the Logos, the Word, to express his presentiments. This also is a fertile soil for all sorts of confusions and substitutions. And this too is reflects a decisive preference for astral fate over spirituality. When the revolutionary turmoil broke out, A. Blok and A. Bely had it not in their powers to manifest a manful activity of spirit, could not make a discernment of spirits, they proved to be wrapped up in the irrational element of the Revolution, flooded with its currents, they passively gave in and attempted to see in the Revolution the "It", with which they waited to meet. But is this an appearance of that which for so long they waited in a passive condition, what they had presentiments of still back then, when at the beginning of the century they espied new horizons? How so very tempting, so very comforting! Finally something great has happened, the mysterious element has unfolded, powerless to be resisted. This then -- is the eternally feminine element, wise in its profundity, the sophianic element. It seems formless only at first glance, merely for the rationalistic consciousness. It is necessary to await from it the truth and beauty of new life. It is amazing, that the "Russian school-boys" (I use Dostoevsky's expression) display not a manly active attitude towards the feminine principle, but rather one that is femininely-passive.

A. Bely constantly all the time mixes up and identifies the "revolution of spirit" with the external, the socio-political revolution. A. Blok does the same. And here in this is a great lie and a temptation, which has to be exposed. This -- is an Anti-Christ substitute. In the introductory article to Issue № 1 of "Epopeya",[1] A. Bely chatters here that: "Christ is inscribed upon the proletarian "I": the ideology of the proletariat -- is the ideology of the unrecognisable Christian Paul, rising up equally against both the Christianity of Peter and against the bourgeois "I", seeking to hold the monopoly on the freedom of Christ". And further on he declares, that the revolution of spirit is a transition from the person, always hedged in and limited, to the collective, "to the collective individualism and to the heroic cosmism, having clearly cut its way through to the

---

[1] *trans. note*: "from French "épopée", a word deriving from the Greek, signifying "epic narrative" or suchlike. "Эпопея" was a 1922 Moscow-Berlin literary journal under editorship of A. Bely, of perhaps only the 1st issue of 285 pages.

proletarian culture". The revolution of spirit is to be disclosed via the class revolution. The Christianity of Paul -- is a class Christianity. But what such is the proletariat, is this an economic category and does it signify the class of factory workers or, perhaps, is this a spiritual category? A. Bely bases his justification of the Revolution upon a play of words and ambiguities. Upon the proletarian "I" can be inscribed Christ only in the instance, if it surmounts its own "proletarianness". "Proletarianness" and bourgeoisness" stand opposite each the other, these are two sides of one and the same spiritual malady. When the proletarian finds himself in most "proletarian" a state, he is malicious, envious and vengeful, and Christ is not in him. But a worker cannot find himself in such a "proletarian" condition, and then have it possible for Christ to live in him. Christ is inscribed only within the human "I", and not in the proletarian or the bourgeois. But the revolution of spirit, which A. Bely awaits, ought evidently to surmount and abolish man, to replace him by the supra-human collective. This too is a temptation of the Anti-Christ. Within Christ the man, the human person is saved and safeguarded for eternal life, whereas in the Anti-Christ the human person perishes and is replaced by the inhuman collective. Herein is that revolution of spirit, which would destroy the human visage and replace it with an inhuman collective, and we as Christians, faithful to the religion of the God-Man and God-manhood, have to oppose it. This is a revolution, directed at the destruction of the eternal foundations of existence, and it -- is anti-ontological. Within the creativity of A. Bely it is man that perishes, it is not humanism, which ought to be surmounted, but rather man, the image and likeness of God, and A. Bely is in agreement with this perishing, he sees in it the arising of a new life, a new consciousness. He surrenders man to the lacerations of cosmic energies and cosmic spirits. He values in anthroposophy also that for him man should appear as a transitory moment of cosmic evolution. It is a cosmic Sophia, and not the Divine Sophia, and it substitutes for and takes the place of Christ, and therefore it has ceased to see man in God. In place of the Divine image of man everywhere instead there have appeared masks.

    The Russian literature of the last decade is striking in its very remarkable manifestations of ontological depravity, dissolution and disintegration of existence. The cosmic whirlwinds have blown apart within them the image of man, the image of the world, the image of God, from every stable aspect of being. This -- is not a moral, but rather an ontological depravity. And there arises upon this soil a false pseudo-

THE CRISIS OF ART

mysticism. Genuine mysticism is a communion with God, a penetrating down to the depths of spiritual life, to the verymost real, the verymost vital. Contemporary mysticism, the kind bound up with contemporary literary currents, has transformed itself into spheres of the crises of man and the crises of culture, of a dissociation of being, and it but reflects the tragic fate of the soul of modern man, as something merely astral. There is an indicator of spiritual incapacity in this terrible mystical self-conceit of contemporary poets and writers. We live in an epoch of a false transvaluation of the mystical significance of art. Too many a poet of our times makes pretense with being endowed of mystical experience and mystical foresights, and they look down upon all the rest of mankind. But in actuality it is easier for a simple mortal to commune a mystical experience, than for modern poets, with people given to a simplicity of heart least of all can there be a duplicitous aspect, least of all murky. The poetic and the mystical experience differ qualitatively. A. Bely and A. Blok make pretense to a mystical acceptance and a mystical comprehension of the Revolution. But this is merely a poetic affection with them, with them least of all can there be found a discerning in the spirits of the Revolution, since they themself are in the grip of its whirlwind elements, whereof they are bereft of freedom of spirit. In the reminiscences of A. Bely can be sensed the spirit of an unhealthy literary coterie, the spirit of having risen to the top of one's small circle. The reverse side of these literateurs in their coterie is a bowing before "the people", before its mysteriousness and authenticity. And thus usually it occurs. The religious misunderstanding and self-conceit of A. Bely and A. Blok is rooted first of all in this, that they await a revelation of the Third Testament, the revelation of Sophia, a revelation of the Spirit, without having accepted the First and Second Testaments. They rend apart time and eternity, the past, the present and the future, and they surrender themself to the false idol of the future. They are pessimists in regards to the past and rosey-red optimists in regards to the future. This makes their mysticism, in essence, areligious and anti-religious. Religion is a connection, a finding of kinship and affinity, a surmounting of the rift between the past and the future, the inclusion of every sundered moment into eternity, the resuscitation of venerable forebearers. They however want to remain within the revolutionary fracture betwixt the past and the future. Revolutionaryness is always anti-religious, since it is contrary to the establishing of connections and affinity in eternity between the past and the future. The mystical intoxication with the revolutionaries, i.e. with processes within time, with the sundering of all connections, is always anti-religious. A. Bely does not know the Hypostasis of the Father, to him as though foreign is the experience of a reverent veneration, i.e. a significant part of the religious experience. He draws upon his own spiritually "proletarian" descent of lineage at the point, when a Christian ought to draw upon his own spiritually-aristocratic descent of lineage, i.e. to feel a connection with the Hypostasis of the Father. Herein is why he thinks, that a revolution of spirit, a creative birth of new life, can be accomplished through destruction, through hatred and malice in regards to everything of the Father. But the genuine miracle of the transfiguration of our sinful and woesome life would be in this, if in the world there should be made a revolution of love. And it is only Christians that await it. Marx made the declaration, that through evil can be realised good in the world, that malice and hate is the path to an utmost social harmony, and after him have followed enormous masses of mankind. Christians however cannot accept this path. But A. Bely and A. Blok are not Christians, they are only Sophians, they bow before the cosmic elements, and for them this has proven acceptable. But it is in vain that all mystically accepting of the Revolution think, that they are maximalists. No, they are rather minimalists, they adapt themselves to the necessary and fatal processes of history, they move along the line of least resistance. It would be proper to term maximalists those, who by the power of their own spirit oppose the elements, the masses, the inevitable movements, and who are spiritually faithful to this, that it is possible not to be vanquished in the future. Fidelity to a vanquished past can be a greater maximalism, than subservience towards a triumphant future. In an exclusively revolutionary striving towards the future always there is an insufficiency of nobility, there is infidelity, the absence of a religious reverence. With Vl. Solov'ev there was both a religious reverence, and a fidelity to the sanctities of the fathers, and a noble resistance to "the spirit of the times". Which is why both A. Blok and A. Bely have little in common with him. They have replaced the veneration of Sophia as God-manhood with the veneration of Sophia as a cosmic element, not divine and not human.

The Revolution has transpired in the spirit of Chernyshevsky, and not in the spirit of Vl. Solov'ev. And it is impossible in any way to combine Vl. Solov'ev with Lavrov, as A. Bely hints at doing. The Revolution is begotten of a century-long process, and in the lineage of this movement we find Belinsky, Bakunin, Chernyshevsky, Dobroliubov, Mikhailovsky,

THE CRISIS OF ART

Lavrov, Plekhanov, Lenin, but we do not find Chaadayev, Khomyakov, Kireevsky, Aksakov, Gogol, Tiutchev, Dostoevsky, Vl. Solov'ev, K. Leont'ev. All these, our most important, are consigned to the "reaction". This indeed is something necessary to ponder. The revolutionaries -- are "socratics" in that contemptuous, that Nietzschean sense, in which A. Bely and A. Blok employ this word. The Revolution in its essence is rationalism taken to the extreme. Extreme socialism and extreme anarchism -- are rationalistic systems taken to the extreme. Russian Bolshevism is a rationalistic folly taken to the limit. Revolutionism always is inspired not only by a thirst for destruction, but also by a misguided will towards an ultimate rationalisation of society, towards a perfect order, towards an organised collective mentality. Revolutionism does not want to know of the organic-irrational forces in society, although it itself is manifest as an irrational force. In this is the antinomic aspect of Revolution. A. Blok and A. Bely, bound up with Scythianism and the Left SR's, represent a final transformation of Russian Populism. But the deeply-engrained lie of Populism rests in this, that it worships the element of the masses in place of the soul, quantity in place of quality. Populism is the offspring begotten of the Intelligentsia consciousness and the Intelligentsia frame of mind. For this consciousness and this frame of mind the People is a mystery, and within this mystery lies concealed truth, is hidden God, and before this mystery one mustneeds bow. This -- is an heteronomous, and not autonomous a condition. At its basis lies the impotence to sense oneself as of the People and in one's own depths to discern God and truth. Vagueness and the "inaudible" in one's own depths is projected from within outwards, into the element of the People. And for those, aware of themselves as of the People, Populism is bereft of all meaning. Truth, new life, God are all revealed in one's own depths, which is of the People, at a supra-personal depth.

The reminiscences concerning A. Blok have not reached their conclusion, and the tragic fate of A. Blok has not been revealed by A. Bely. It is difficult to say, how he will do this, if he finishes with his reminiscences. But the fate of A. Blok -- is very significant and remarkable a fate. In it there has transpired the tragic ruin of the false sophianic romanticism, there has been exposed its inward impotence. And the "Beauteous Lady" is not real, not ontological for A. Blok. There is not even a remote sense of contact with an existing Sophia here. Everything is submerged in a murky and ambiguous atmosphere. And there is no spiritual resistance against this murkiness and ambiguity. "Balaganchik" ["The Puppet Show", 1905], a very remarkable piece by A. Blok, is the ruination of the "Beauteous Lady". It exposes the non-reality, the inauthenticity, the non-ontologic aspect of everything. The darkness spreads within the soul of A. Blok. But here hardly a year before death has once again appeared the spectre of the "Beauteous Lady", of Sophia, in a sinister and unprecedented guise. He beheld Her in the image of the Russian Revolution. Here the image of Sophia becomes submerged in a final murkiness and there perishes all aspect of accepting the image as Divine. A. Blok fiercely, and by death, paid for his hallucination, for the dreadful mistake, to which he had given himself. He writes the "The Twelve" ["Dvenadtsat'",1918], a piece amazing and almost of genius, better, than what he had written about the Revolution. In the "The Twelve" is given a genuine image of the Russian Revolution with all its terrible viciousness, but its duplicity and equivocation reach the point of sacrilege. Here A. Blok indulges himself taking terrible license with the figure of Christ. The romantic and dreamy sophianism of A. Blok failed to open to him the path to perceiving the image and countenance of Christ. Through Christ only can there be overcome the temptation of duplicity of thought. After this life A. Blok submerges himself into an ultimate gloom. Again there grows dark for him the image of the "Beauteous Lady", and he remains before an abyss of desolation. He dies off of a spiritual sickness, from his engulfing gloom of soul and non-belief. A. Blok -- is of an unbelieving soul, all his life languishing for faith. He caught sight the deceptive flashes, the mirages in the desert and yet failed to see the true dawn. And thus in his tragic fate is exposed the lie of all this path, of all this current in Russian spiritual life. Literature had a presentiment of the Revolution, and the Revolution in literature transpired earlier, than in life. But one can only be called a prophet, if one rises above those elements, about which one prophesies. After his death A. Blok was crowned a foremost Russian poet, and justly so. A poet however is not obligated to be a spiritual teacher and prophet, but blameworthy are those, who want to make him so.

Nikolai Berdyaev. (1923)

The Liege-Knight of Poverty
(Léon Bloy)

"Lord Jesus, Thou prayest for those, who crucify Thee, and Thou dost crucify those, who do love Thee!"

The translator expresses his profoundest gratitude to
Lisa Holsberg
In locating this hitherto rare Berdyaev text!

The Liege-Knight of Poverty (Léon Bloy)

(1914 - 176)¹

"Bloy n'a qu'une ligne, et cette ligne est son contour. Cette ligne, c'est l'Absolu dans la pensée, l'Absolu dans la parole, dans les actes. Absolu tel que tout en lui est indentique. Lorsqu'il vomit sur un contemporain, c'est, infiniment et exactement, comme s'il chantait la gloire de Dieu. C'est pourquoi la gloire de ce monde lui est refusee".

"Bloy consists of a single line, and this line follows along the same contour. This line -- is the Absolute, the Absolute in thought, the Absolute in words, the Absolute in comportment. Everything is identically absolute for him. And when he spews forth venom against some contemporary, it is with the same exactitude and fervour, as though he be chanting to the glory of God. Wherefore the glory of this world is refused him".

Henry de Groux [1866-1930]

I.

In France, the old Latin culture has reached its final refinement and its autumnal blossoming. This culture by its blood is connected with Catholicism. Barbey d'Aurevilly [Jules, 1808-1889], and Hello [Ernest, 1828-1885], Villiers de l'Isle-Adam [August, 1838-1889], Verlaine [Paul, 1844-1896], Huysmans [Joris-Karl, 1848-1907] -- are the final sort Catholics, the final sparks of the fading Catholic spirit, the final flowerings of the waning Latin culture. This sort of *rafinement* (refinement) was

---

¹ RYTSAR' NISCHETY (Léon Bloy). First published in journal "Sophiya", P. P. Muratov editor, Moscow, 1914, №. 6, p. 49-78.

First reprint of this Berdyaev article is within its incorporation (p.10-50) into the book, entitled "Кровь бедняка" ("Blood of the Beggar"), Russkii Put', Moscow, 2005, 288 pages. Text includes the first translation from French into Russian from L. Bloy's works "Le Sang du pauvre", "Exégèse des lieux communs", "L'Âme de Napoléon", and a brief "Forward" by N. Struve.

possible only in the France of the XIX and XX Centuries, in which was revealed the decadent loftiness, the final bounds of the hyper-cultural Latinism, so often in betrayal to Catholicism and in revolt against it, but by its flesh and blood invariably belonging to its spirit. And this -- is sensual a spirit, of a plasticity in its religiousness, not torn away from the flesh, from the historical and the concrete, from the aesthetic aspects. Latin Catholicism reveals itself as exceptional and unprecedented within the history of the producing of artistry, with a plasticity of perfection and finish, aesthetically impacting the soul. This aesthetic force of the perfective architecture of the Catholic Church was sensed with an especial acuity by the final Catholics of the XIX Century, the decadents of delicate and refined a culture. These renegades, individualists, uncompromising, lived under the magic spell of the beauty of composition of the Catholic Church. The entirety of the Latin culture had been engendered from the Catholic spirit, from the Catholic Christianity and the Catholic paganism, and the path, along which Catholicism took this culture, was not by way of a spiritual immersion within, of a spiritual freedom and boldness. Upon this path rather was a plasticity of attachment to the external world, towards everything materially an object. Within the bosom of the Latin culture, every spiritual and religious impulse of renewal assumes the form of a return to Catholicism, whereby the spirit is constrained and it is not thus a faith, wherein that "the spirit doth spirit, whithersoever it doth will" [Cf. Jn. 3:8]. And all the boldness of these returned Catholics becomes directed upon a fiery denunciation of the bourgeois world, such as has apostacised from and betrayed the ancient Truth, the ancient Beauty. The boldness of a creative initiative within religious life is neither there in Barbey d'Aurevilly, nor in Hello, nor in Villiers de l'Isle-Adam, nor in Huysmans. For them the spiritual life is the Catholic life in accord with the Papacy and the Inquisition. Everything revolutionary and of revolt in them is directed against the bourgeois world, its having forsaken Catholicism. All these people -- are revolutionary a sort of reactionaries, wounded by the bourgeois ugliness and untruth, they are oriented towards the past and prophesying about the past. And these people lived out their life in poverty and obscurity. In their uncompromising attitude towards the bourgeois world there was an unique sort of heroism, a new sort heroism comprised of aesthetes and decadents. André Gide [1869-1951] in an hostile article on Villiers de l'Isle-Adam says: "Baudelaire [Charles, 1821-1867], Barbey d'Aurevilly, Hello, Bloy, Huysmans. All have one trait in common:

THE CRISIS OF ART

an ingratitude towards life and even an hatred towards life -- contempt, shame, terror, disdain, and in all aspects -- a sort of religious spitefulness towards life. The ironic tone of Villiers towards this is the result" ("Prétextes"). This uncompromising inflexibility, this horror at the ugliness and vileness would thus have to seem to the bourgeois modern sort a denial of life.

    The final and most significant figure in this cultural current was Léon Bloy [1846-1917], regarding as his teachers Barbey d'Aurevilly and Hello, nigh close to Villiers de l'Isle-Adam and Verlaine, and an affinity with Carlyle. In this unappreciated and almost unknown writer[1] are the features of genuine genius. This is a man of new a spirit, of new a spiritual formation -- both connected with his predecessors, and yet deeply distinct from them. Léon Bloy -- is a man of strength, and not weakness, and in this he is infinitely distinct from Huysmans, of whom he is unjustly not fond of and neither has acknowledged, though in much there has to be sensed an affinity with him. In the person of Léon Bloy the dying Latin-Catholic culture has evidenced an almost prophetic power and fiery passion. The tragedy of the Latin spirit has reached in L. Bloy a final intensity. The decline of Catholicism, the decay of the Latin culture is something that L. Bloy himself makes mention of frequently. He well knows: that what he loves, what his spirit ineffably is connected with, is passing into decline and dying. And yet all the same, as a true Latin, as a romantic, he will not allow for a spiritual life and religious renewal outside of Catholicism, apart from submission to the Pope, apart from all the perfect plasticity, all the architectural wonders of the Catholic Church. All the Latin tragedy of L. Bloy consists in this, as how to experience the religious power within the powerlessness of Catholicism, a religious fidelity in the religious betrayal of Catholicism, the religious beauty in the religious ugliness of Catholicism; how to be a religious prophet, whilst remaining oriented towards the Catholic past. The Latin spirit, powerless to experience Christianity as inward a mystery of the spirit, would as such have to come nigh the tragic despondency of Léon Bloy, amidst the unbearable torment

---

    [1] Not a single line of L. Bloy has previously been rendered into the Russian language. All that is here proffered is my translation. (N. Berdyaev note). [*trans. note*: a situation of obscurity that remained until 2005, with publication of the "Кровь бедняка" source-text, from which our English translation is made].

of his life, in order finally to find some way out of this. And thus the same with the tragic attitude of L. Bloy towards France. He religiously believes in France, he confesses a French messianism; for him the sufferings of France -- are the sufferings of God Himself. And to him everything hateful about modern France, all -- the ugliness and the stench, all -- reflects a forsaking and betrayal. For L. Bloy thus there has not remained the final consolation of being a romantic and aesthete, and in suchlike a manner to beat a retreat from life. He is split off from this typical wont of the romantic and the aesthete. He represents instead -- a tragic realism. He is a prophet beneathe the malicious mask of the pamphleteer. From him sound forth apocalyptic notes. By the forceful power of his language, the originality, the intensity, the fiery and measured delineations L. Bloy -- proves exceptional a writer, indeed singularly so. He can be compared with our K. Leont'ev, a writer of acute genius, and partly also with Nietzsche, but better that he not be compared with him. The titles of his books as such, and the terminology of chapter headings -- is a stroke of genius. And such blazing and scorching a sharp-mindedness and sarcasm I have never elsewhere encountered within world literature. His -- is a most radical and uncompromising spirit, living always in the Absolute and by the Absolute.

Letters of Barbey d'Aurevilly and Léon Bloy have been published. L. Bloy has been very fond of Barbey d'Aurevilly, has regarded him as his teacher, and himself the inheritor of his spirit. But in the correspondence it is clearly apparent, how remote L. Bloy is from the romanticism of Barbey d'Aurevilly, how far removed he is from his urbaneness, from his levity, from the possibility of aesthetic consolations. In certain of the letters, Barbey d'Aurevilly provides a sharp and measured consideration of L. Bloy, who was then still a young man, and just beginning to write. Barbey d'Aurevilly sensed L. Bloy -- to be a man of different a generation, of different a spirit, of different a time. For him is no longer possible a sense of playfulness, he is no longer still a romantic, he -- is a realist in the most profound sense of this word; his sharp-wittedness, inevitable in a Frenchman, does not provide easy a sense of joy. Barbey d'Aurevilly perceived Léon Bloy as boundlessly serious. His seriousness gives rise to indignation and wrath. This -- is a serious man, sensing the onset of the end, the proximity to the limit. He sees everything in exaggerated a manner, since only in the exaggerated manner is it possible to closely peer at much. "This Your manner of seeing, I know this well, -- writes Barbey d'Aurevilly, -- where everything is seen in enormity. Inside the nature of

THE CRISIS OF ART

Your mind everything is seen as large... In both the good and the bad your eyes tend to magnify the object" ("Lettres de J. A. Barbey d'Aurevilly à Léon Bloy"). L. Bloy does not know a measure of moderation in the perception of things, and for a perceiving of the boundaries and the end-points, perhaps, one mustneeds transcend every measure. "You have a serious and strong imagination, and when it gets going, it readily gets terrible. You have the scowering black brows talent... Your tone gets monotonous (perhaps, too much so). *You get monotonous, as well as serious and deep* (Italics mine -- N. B.). I would wish You be more balanced. You have a rare trait: *an assuredness* (Italics mine -- N. B.), an assuredness beyond saying... And yet still, what is in You and what it is impossible to sufficiently admire in a man of Your cold generation, is -- *this enthusiasm* (Italics mine -- N. B.)" (Ibid.). This characterisation is amazingly insightful and penetrating: as proven by all the life and all the creativity of L. Bloy -- always serious, deep, assured, an enthusiast, having devoted himself all and entirely to the Solely One. And thus L. Bloy was also perceived and acknowledged by this final romantic, Barbey d'Aurevilly, one of the greatest writers of France in the XIX Century. He gives a brilliant summation of L. Bloy's style. "You are at the same time glittering both bright and dark. You are like a ruby glimmering with dark flaws; but the dark specks dominate the red ruby: something akin to a bit of black velvet on fire!" (Ibid.). Léon Bloy -- is a fiery and black sort of writer. In his antinomic manner of writing there is a refined crudeness. His books are transfused with a genial sort of abusive scoldings, which never assume bad a tone. Someone whom he has thus berated, could not of course forgive him this, and he has berated almost everyone, and still we can only but find delight in this dazzling gift of scolding, this eternal creativeness of a dressing-down demolition, the almost unconveyable crude expressions, always extraordinarily acidic. With L. Bloy there is always a single tone, but in this tone of a blazing fiery blackness there is a congenial acidity, yet never irksome. Only in France could a L. Bloy appear, only there could be possible the appearing of the ultimate such acerbity of the Latin spirit. But the France of the XIX and XX Centuries does not know the like of such a seriousness and depth, such absoluteness in everything, such a prophetic gift, hid behind the foul frown of the pamphetist, and cannot indeed properly appreciate such a phenomenon. In German culture completely impossible would be the incisiveness of L. Bloy, his congenial paradoxical aspect and his crudeness, his unenlightened sort of French subtle decadence, and hence he would prove there intolerable.

Barbey d'Aurevilly prepared the path for the possibility of the appearing of L. Bloy. But Bloy's style is not romantically that of the old France, deriving from the Middle Ages. In it there is no longer still the old elegance, the aristocratic mannerisms, the stylistic fidelity to historical traditions. L. Bloy was born at a time then, when it was impossible still to be a romantic, and was born suchlike, that he could not still be an aesthete, although he loves beauty passionately and intensely. The attitude of modern Catholicism towards beauty is painful for L. Bloy and arouses indignation within him, in excess of the obligatory bounds of obedience for a Catholic. "The modern sort Catholics hate art with an hatred wild, horrid and unaccountable. Without doubt, it is not very much loved, this poor hapless art, within modern society, and I am forever endlessly repeating this... But everywhere -- is shallow a contempt towards beauty, and among certain Catholics -- an actual abhorrence" ("Un brelan d'excommuniés" [1889]). "They are frightened of beauty, as though it be an alluring occasion for sin, as a very sin itself, and an audacity of genius frightens them, as though it be of the hand of Lucifer. They entrust their pious wisdom in a banishing of the great" (Ibid.). These words, so tragic from the lips of a faithful Catholic, for whom outside Catholicism there be no spiritual life, indeed there be no beauty, were written by him in a book about the Catholics Barbey d'Aurevilly, E. Hello and Verlaine, excommunicated as such and not acknowledged by the Catholic world. And for the bourgeois Catholicism, according to the way Bloy puts it, Barbey d'Aurevilly was *l'enfant terrible* (an unruly vexation), E. Hello -- was *le fou* (a fool), Verlaine -- *le lépreux* (a virtual leper). L. Bloy cannot forgive papism its persecution against beauty, genius and talent. He harshly and angrily rails against the Church for its non-acknowledgement of Barbey d'Aurevilly, whom he regards as a great Catholic writer. He is indignant, that for the Church, Verlaine was viewed as merely a simple convert and that in him was not recognised a great Christian poet. From him burst forth admissions terrible for a Catholic, -- that the Catholic Church itself would fail to acknowledge Christ, were He to appear again on earth. It does not acknowledge anything too exalted, exceeding the average level. When Bloy once said to a certain hierarch, that in E. Hello there were genuine insights to be garnered, that worthy curtly replied to him, that

THE CRISIS OF ART

with Bl. Augustine[1] and Thomas Aquinas had been said everything worth saying, and that thus there was no need for any insights from E. Hello. And hence Bloy sensed likewise, that the official Catholic world had no need of him also, of his prophetic power, of his fidelity to the point of blood, of his chivalrant knightly service to the Church of Christ. His most grievous wounds were inflicted him by Catholics, by his co-religionists. In them he was met with a monstrously icy cold indifference and inattention. Only among foreigners, people of a different faith did he sometimes encounter, and true very rarely so, with human an attention.[2] He was a solitary figure in the bourgeois world, but even more terrible was that he has been a solitary figure within the Catholic world. He has lived the cult of the great, of heroism and of genius. The great, along with heroism and genius, are needful neither for the bourgeois world, nor for the Catholic world, having so accommodated itself to the bourgeois world. L. Bloy has gone as a solitary upon life's path, and there is a sad grandeur in this solitary going along not as an individualist, but rather as a Catholic, faithful to the point of death. Léon Bloy -- is singular in his sort of the appearance of an unlimited aloneness, of a forsakenness and being ignored within Catholicism. The fate of L. Bloy has to be seen in comparison with the fate of Nietzsche. Nietzsche was a religious blindman, L. Bloy -- is a religious seer. Both experienced infinite an aloneness and forsakenness. But the aloneness and forsakenness of a faithful Christian, all his life pronouncing his inherent faith, is indeed the more terrible fate.

---

[1] *trans. note*: Surprising perhaps to some, but St. Augustine is ranked among the Saints in the Orthodox Church, for which accrue various titles indicative of spiritual exploit leading to sainthood. Thus, among the Orthodox both St. Augustine and St. Jerome are accorded the title of "*Blessed*", which in useage becomes abbreviated as "*Bl*".

[2] Such as when he met with the help and attention of Pr. Usurov [Aleksandr Ivanovich, 1843-1900], a reknown legal advocate, and connoisseur appreciative of French literature [in 1891 defending L. Bloy against charges of "defamation"].

Nicholas Berdyaev

II.

The diary of L. Bloy, bearing the title -- "Le mendiant ingrat" ("The Indigent Ingrate"), is a striking and unusual book. In its laying bare the soul, in its laying bare the intimate impacts of fate, this book can be compared with the "Uedinennoe" ("Solitaria") and "Opavshie list'ya" ("Fallen Leaves") of Rozanov. There is a formal affinity both in the laying bare of intimacies, and in an audacity to say that, about which people never dare say. But the soul of L. Bloy is dissimilar to the soul of Rozanov. The soul of L. Bloy is exceptionally manly, strong, fiery, ardent in abasement and self-abasement. His ill-tempered manner itself, and L. Bloy was an exceptionally ill-tempered writer, was experienced in his soul as a sort of Christian fidelity. Léon Bloy lived his life in shocking poverty and lack of acknowledgement. He had to live through charity, he was close to death by starvation; there were days, when he had not the wherewithal to light a candle at supper; he had children dying from poverty. And he was forsaken by everyone, former friends abandoned him, all betrayed him. It was considered too unseemly, too disquieting and a bad bet to connect one's fate with such a man. He evoked towards himself a great deal of hatred. He did not make in life a single compromise, did not yield on anything, so as to earn himself his daily bread. He experienced his poverty not only as the outward needfulness and misfortune, but also as an inward fate, the fate of the Christian in the world. He ardently defends his idea of poverty in the world. Christ Himself was poor, and every rightful truth in the world ought thus to be poor. He experiences everything in his fate as something providential, as worldwide, and not subjective nor by chance. And from the lamentations over his suffering-filled life he always passes over to give thanks for his fate and every tribulation sent him by God. With L. Bloy there was a withering contempt towards those, who see only "by chance" there, where ought instead to be seen the workings of Divine Providence. He writes to his friend, the artist Henry de Groux:

"Nous avons été lancés l'un sur l'autre, du fond de l'Eternité, par la main d'un Discobole infaillible, en un point déterminé de la durée, -- pour qu'une chose mystérieuse, infiniment agréable et nécessaire, fut

THE CRISIS OF ART

accomplie sur notre planète. C'est que les manguers d'excréments nomment le "Hasard" ("Le mendiant ingrat").[1]

Henry de Groux characterises L. Bloy in contrast with E. Hello, saying: "I am impelled to say, what Ernest Hello might have written about his friend Léon Bloy. -- Bloy consists of a single line, and this line follows along the same contour. And this line -- is the Absolute. The Absolute in thoughts, the Absolute in words, the Absolute in comportment... And when he spews forth venom against some contemporary, it is with the same exactitude and fervour, as though he be chanting to the glory of God. Wherefore the glory of this world is refused him". Among the few fond of and remembering him have sensed, that he lives in the Absolute and by the Absolute. And he himself sensed this also. "I am almost alone in the world. I might have had, like so many others, numerous friends. With my initial efforts, which in wondrous a manner were noisy an affair, I at once received applause. Those, fond of power, even among the atheists, were with me. I was not yet the author of "Le Désespéré" ("The Desperate"). But when indeed they learned of my path, when it became clear, that I am a man of the Absolute, then no one wanted to be bothered with me" ("Le mendiant ingrat"). One mustneeds also lovingly believe in the exceptional calling of L. Bloy, in order to approve of such an exalted self-appraisal and conveying such an identification of one's own fate with the fate of the Divine in the world. He writes to a certain lady: "You love the downtrodden, but not my sort... The effects of complaining fail to touch your heart... Do you know, that I am one of those people, whose hand is raised against all and against whom all hands are raised" (Ibid.). "God -- is one alone against all. In this is a mystery. It is evident, that a man, be he a criminal, against whom is all the world and who is thus one against all, has in himself something Divine" (Ibid.).[2] A favourite sort thought of Bloy

---

[1] "We have been cast upon one another, from the depths of Eternity, by the unfailing hand of a Discobolos [Discus-thrower], at a fixed point in time, -- for something mysterious, infinitely agreeable and necessary, to be accomplished upon our planet. This is what these excrement eaters term as "Hazardous Chance" ("The Indigent Ingrate").

[2] *trans note*: What a strange observation, which if left unqualified, leads along the psychological paths of Dostoevsky's Raskol'nikov and Kirillov.

Nicholas Berdyaev

-- is this suffering aloneness and forsakenness of God Himself. The aloneness of man can be religiously experienced as an aloneness of the Divine, as God-likeness. In this is the pathos of L. Bloy. The sufferings of God exceed the sufferings of the world and of man. Righteous truth always winds up getting crucified in the world, this is an aspect of the perpetually eternal crucifixion of God, the crucifixion of Christ. And therefore ultimately sweet and of delight are the sufferings and crucifixion in life. With L. Bloy there is always a sense of the destitution and anguished forsakenness of God Himself. And yet this exceptional experience is unique a force. He sees Christ as eternally crucified and it is as though he fails to see the Resurrection. He takes to heart the sufferings of Christ, the poor and destitute Christ. He always calls Christ *Le Pauvre* (the Poor), and for him Christ is foremost of all the Bednyak (Бедняк), the Poor Wretched One, bereft the riches of the world. And L. Bloy himself always has this experience of feeling crucified. This gives him the power to go on living. Wretchedness, forsakenness, crucifixion -- is strange a force, and yet mighty. L. Bloy scorns and hates the rosy, the sentimental Christianity, he scorns and hates every sense of happiness, felicity, and good order. In a moment of extreme need he notices in a dark corner a forgotten sum of thirty-five centimes. "How would Jesus have said it: -- this is all, that I am able of at this very minute. Patience and courage! Do not pity Me. For I do be crucified" ("Pages choisies"). Such an extraordinary sense of Christ is impossible to find in all of Christian literature. Christ, God Himself -- is the poorest of poor wretches; He is forsaken by the world, deprived from Him are the riches of the world, of Him flows the very blood. "First of all and most of all Christ -- is the Forsaken One. Those who love him, ought also to be the forsaken, in likeness to Him, the forsaken by God".[1] (Ibid.). And Léon Bloy thus consigns himself to poverty and forsakenness in the name of Christ. The rich Catholics turn away from him, and he in turn disdains them. He knows, that the joys of wealth have their own connection with the sufferings of the poor. L. Bloy is married to a love of poverty. The wretched poverty relates to Christ. When people receive money, they change and they betray Christ, just like Judas. But how dissimilar is the

---

[1] *trans. note*: Cf. Mt. 27: 46 and Christ's final words on the Cross: "My God, My God, wherefore hast Thou forsaken Me? (Eli, Eli, lema sabachthani)".

THE CRISIS OF ART

voluntary poverty of L. Bloy, in contrast to the betrothal to wretched a life in St. Francis! [1] In a different world period St. Francis made this sort of marriage -- fondly. His poverty is of a sort luminous and blessed. The poverty of L. Bloy -- is gloomy and bloody. The world has gone a far way in its falling away from the Poor One in its quest of money; and the world has become all more and more bourgeois and all ever anew it crucifies Christ. In the bourgeois realm money, cut adrift and separate from the Poor One, results in its own sort of a frightening and terrifying marriage with poverty. The frightful poverty in bourgeois Paris, in the modern bourgeois culture, in much is more terrible, than in the poverty of the beautiful Umbrian valleys of St. Francis or the Thebaid wastelands of old. The experience of L. Bloy -- is a modern sort experience, unknown by the Saints of former ages. Léon Bloy -- is in the mould of the holy fool in modern culture, in bourgeois France. An unprecedented phenomenon. He lives and writes like some holy fool,[2] he transgresses all the norms of bourgeois society. He understands the consequences of humiliation, opens himself to mockery. Like some holy fool, he treats the world as a joke, spewing bile on everything living in the world. L. Bloy declares of himself and his wife: "Ne sommes-nous pas les bohèmes du Saint-Esprit, les vagabonds du Consolateur?" ("Are we not like bohemians of the Holy Spirit, the vagabonds of the Comforter?") (Pages cloisies").

The wolf of despair always gets turned by L. Bloy into a blessing of the fate, an acceptance of the good purpose of everything sent from God. His faith passes through terrible temptations, and it is strong and unshattered, like a slab of granite. He has struggled with God, but has not known scepticism and non-faith. "It is only from these tears (over our Lord Jesus Christ) that I have found an almost beyond-human assurance, needful

---

[1] *trans. note*: This contrast helps substantiate Berdyaev's claim, earlier in our work, that L. Bloy is focused exclusively upon the crucifixion of Christ, and is insensitive to the radical significance of the Resurrection: a psychological trait peculiar to Catholic spirituality and the West. The example of St. Francis tends to echo the words of the St. John Chrysostomos Sermon, heard at the close of the Orthodox Paschal Matins, -- "*Let no one today bewail his poverty!*"...

[2] *trans note*: the "holy fool" (yurodivy (юродивый)) is Russian and Orthodox a phenomenon amongst the rank of Saints.

for me, in order so to suffer, in order to accept my most dreadsome existence, in order never to cease to stand at the foot of the Cross, in darkness and torments" (Le mendiant ingrat"). L. Bloy was nigh close to a final despair, and then he cried out: "Remember O Lord, that I have co-suffered with Thee... Why these horrid sufferings with no way out? Why these hellishly beguiling and jeering privileges of the Word to a man of good will, who has not the possibility to get himself heard? All the same grumbling over the course of ten years and all the same Divine deafness. But my courage doth weaken" (Ibid.). "Now already neither shirts, nor shoes, nor hat nor clothing... Why does God stretch forth His hand upon those, whom He doth love, the gracious hand of goodness and glory?" (Ibid.). "O dreadsome day! No wine nor wholesome food, nor fuel wherewith to cook, all which threatens *human assuredness* in the possibility to tomorrow feed the children, the impossibility to continue living this way and the impossibility to run away and flee, foreseeing forlornness from all the world and the evident hostility of such numerous people; and finally and foremost of all, this endless tormentive expectation of some deliverer, who nonetheless fails to show up; all this brings us to the point of despair. And at the same time as we redouble our hopes, our house shakes from storms and the shrieking of the sky, like as with a death without God. For whom do we so suffer? And still I can work, and write books amidst such torments. About this will be an accounting on the day of the Dread Last Judgement" ("Pages choisies"). And Bloy cries out: "Lord, I have no confidence towards Thee" and pronounces then a God-wrestling prayer, which seems "as though someone might dictate" for him. And sometimes he conveys into the diary suchlike words: "Lord Jesus, Thou prayest for those, who crucify Thee, and Thou dost crucify those, who do love Thee!" L. Bloy belongs to those few, who not only *affamés de pain*, but also *affamés de Beaute d'Infini* (not only hunger for bread, but also hunger for the Beauty of Infinitude). He says on behalf of these people: "They will be persecuted, very likely. Feckless nomads of a great dream, they will wander the earth, like Cain, and will perhaps be compelled the company of wild beasts, in order not to remain without moorage. Kept at bay, like arsonists and repulsive lowlifes, cursed by women with their sensual glances, who see in them merely tramps, surrounded by children and dogs, in the terror of sixty years wanton of happiness, bedraggled by the music of final a while, -- towards the end they will agonise in such fetid dumps, that even the maggots and dung beetles will shun their corpses" ("Pages choisies"). In these words there is a genuine rapture, an ecstatic sense of abandon, of forlornness, unacceptance, aloneness. L. Bloy experiences this condition as something sent from God, as a condition of God Himself. He experiences not only grief and torment, that all should abandon and betray him, but also a genuine ecstasy at the common hatred towards him. This reinforces in him the sense of his own exceptional and great calling, his as it were Divine anointing. He never experiences rejection and aloneness as resultant of sin, but always as a sign of his own calling, his own vocation. His aggressive and to the end manly spirit does not know balance and reflection. He despises any analytic approach, such as might sap the masculine wholeness of spirit. "The man, around whom spread catastrophes, -- is a select chosen man. Woe to that one, whose presence but rearranges atoms" ("Le mendiant ingrat"). And he sense himself as such a select chosen man. But this exceptional faith in himself is also aligned with his faith in God. The faith in himself and the faith in God -- in him is one monolithic faith. Inherent to L. Bloy is an extraordinary sense of individualness, of individual unrepeatability.[1] "The person, the human individualness, inscribed and imprinted upon each person, and sometimes so imposingly upon the visage of a great man, is something quite sacred, something fore-ordained towards the Universal Resurrection, to eternal life, to the blessed uniting. The countenance, the visage of each man -- is altogether an unique entry way into Paradise, and which it is impossible to confuse with others and through which will enter in one soul" ("Pages choisies"). The sense of God for him is inseparable from the sense of individualness.

The moments of despair and hopelessness for L. Bloy are always surmounted by a great submissiveness to God, and to giving thanks for everything. He has some remarkable words on prayer. "It is necessary to pray. Everything else is vanity and stupidity. It is necessary to pray, in order to bear the vileness of this world; it is necessary to pray, in order to be pure; it is necessary to pray, in order to receive the power to wait. Not from despair, nor from black sorrow for a man, within whom much gets prayed. This I tell you, and with much authority!... It is necessary to pray simply, randomly, but with mighty an intent. It is necessary to pray as one

---

[1] *trans note*: the unique "unrepeatability" of each person is likewise constant a Berdyaev theme.

ought, patiently, not subject to vexation nor distraction, until perchance one experiences a special stirring with a feeling of fire in the soul. Then one can calmly go and put up with whatever" ("Le mendiant ingrat"). L. Bloy has put up with hellish a life, since he has prayed much and boundlessly had faith. He writes to Henry de Groux: "*Everything, that happens, I give thanks for*, I accept this with all authority regarding my poverty, which is as perfect, as God is perfect, and which therefore itself is to be blessed... If for us there be not money sufficing, this means, that the money would have been to the ruination of us". When L. Bloy lost his final source of earnings from a newspaper, for having defended Tailhade [Laurent, 1854-1919], whom everyone was in an uproar over, and by this doomed himself to two years of poverty, he then exclaimed: "Shouts of jubilation, a rapture of happiness in my home! The peeling of bells in the hearts! Let's lay a table for the festive feast of poverty" ("Le mendiant ingrat"). He lifts to God a prayer of poverty: "I pray Thee, my God, and humbly do I beseech to accept me into the number of some few poor, whom Thou doth employ unto Thy Glory, when Thine Wondrous Visage shalt array the battle fallen" ("Les dernières collones de l'Eglise"). And towards the Catholic clergy he addresses the words: "You, Messieurs, heirs of the Apostles, I implore not to disdain a poor wretch, a seeker of Christ, and neither hate the artists and poets, nor cast away into the hostile camp those, who should most of all want to fight alongside you and for you" ("Pages choisies"). L. Bloy foremost of all regarded himself a faithful Catholic. This was with a tragic sense of self. "A loathing most terrible, most intractable, most insidious has come over me on the part of my brother Catholics... None of these Pharisees has come to me in help, nor wanted to ascertain, whether I do falter under the burden of woes, cold and hungry" ("Le mendiant ingrat"). L. Bloy was not given to learn the joy of a Christian interaction. And indeed to whom is it given without the conditional rhetoric? L. Bloy -- is the by-birth and by-blood sort of Catholic, without the inward turnabout, without a religious sort of growth. He neither understands nor loves the anew converted, the anew returned. Towards Huysmans he is terribly unjust, cannot forgive him his weakness, accuses him of hatred towards everything great, healthy, strong. The conversion of literary figures of the sort of Paul Bourget [1852-1935], François Coppée [1842-1908], and Ferdinand Brunetière (1849-1906), he regarded as a final blow, inflicted the Church. The salon sort Catholicism was for him a matter of contempt and disgust. The conversion of François

THE CRISIS OF ART

Coppée was for him merely an indication, that Christianity had become frivolous a matter. He speaks heatedly about the watering-down and decay of Catholicism. Bristling with anger he speaks about the ruination of medieval heroism and the arising of the pomaded and contrived salon Catholicism of St. Francis de Sales. And very incisive is his judgement on the Jesuits. He sees in this that the Jesuits have introduced analysis and have begotten a total psychologism, disjunctive and dissolute in its effect. The Jesuit method leads to a contemplation of one oneself, in place of a contemplation of God. And consequently from the Church vanish the Saints. "Flee such analysis, as one would flee the Devil, and recourse to God, like one in peril of drowning" (Ibid.). L. Bloy -- dwells in the absolute, the Jesuits -- in the relative and conditional. Léon Bloy -- is an exceptional phenomenon within Catholicism: he is an out of step renegade, a rebel within Catholicism. His connection with historical Catholicism is incomprehensible and antinomic. In the Catholic Church there is no sensing of the Poor One and there is not the poverty, the wretchedness; it has instead become subordinated to bourgeoisness, to money, to a disavowal of Christ.

In the suffering and intolerable life of L. Bloy, besides his extraordinary faith in himself and in God, there was still one other source of light -- his wife, a northerner of Danish extract, a being still more heroic and able, than was he himself. In dedicating the "Pages choisies" to his wife, L. Bloy says: "She fell in love with me, because I spoke to her about God; she entered into marriage with me, because it was said to her, that I am poor". And he concludes the dedication with the words, that concerning their tragic life "it will be told of, my dear Zhanna [Johanna], in the future life". The pages of the diary dedicated to her are very insightful, and filled with love. A basic and rather bizarre contradiction in the life of L. Bloy was this, that he had a family and children. Yet he did not have to be the typical sort of man. His wife transformed this strange life of poverty and forsakenness into a Divine mystery. All was transformed into beauty in their union. To the wife of L. Bloy belongs the pervading insights of thought and finding ways out into the light during the moments of hopelessness. Only with her could he remain a pilgrim wanderer upon the earth. And beautiful and enlightening the same, is everything that he writes about his children. But in him himself there is something not so beautiful, almost ugly. Someone has said, that he has hands like an hunchback. A strange mixture of arrogance with pettiness, of self-assuredness with a sick spiteful streak. A peculiar fate: a proud man in perpetual humiliation, and self-abasing, like a fool. In the pages of his diary he does not spare himself, in baring everything about himself in ugly detail. A great strength in L. Bloy is witnessed to in this, that after a terrible life filled with humiliation and sufferings he has not fallen into pessimism, and indeed despises pessimism. "There is nothing in the world, that makes me so want to vomit (vomisse), as pessimism, which as such encompasses all the possible forms of impotence: a powerlessness of mind, of the will, of the heart, of the night-time and digestion. Had I the honour to command in a time of war, I would shoot down the pessimists, like they shoot down the spies and deserters. I esteem but immeasurable a valour, and I -- I will never admit myself beaten!" ("Le mendiant ingrat").

III.

L. Bloy has two novels -- "Le Désespéré" and "La Femme pauvre" ("The Desperate" and "The Woman Who was Poor"). These novels have autobiographical a character and are very interesting as to the traits of his person. Within them are some penetrating thoughts, and there are some very successful places. But Bloy has no specific talent as a novelist, no sort of plots, no artistic phantasies; his novels are monotonous and can prove trite for anyone, not interested in the person of Bloy. Everything, that L. Bloy writes, -- is about himself. His manner of writing cannot be ascribed to any defined gendre. His literary giftedness is enormous and exceptionally original. But his writing lacks artistry, fails as art. In the creativity of L. Bloy he experiences himself, the subject, as the world, as the object. And therefore written by L. Bloy transgresses the bounds of every canon of creativity, of every canon of thought, of every canon of art. L. Bloy is from those, for whom it can be said, that he exists, and everything wrought by him is merely a disclosure from his entire being, a being unrepeatable in its uniqueness. Impossible it is to make an approach towards him with any sort of canonical critique, nor with any sort of normative demands, typically applicable to thought or artistry. It is necessary to either accept or to reject him as an existing phenomenon. And in L. Bloy's violation of every cultural protocol there is a manifestation of audacious power. His life he did not deign to live within the norms of bourgeois society (bourgeoisness as a metaphysical category), the bourgeois world had disdained him, and his creativity did not fit into the framework of the norms of bourgeois culture, did not subordinate it to any sort of canon. He transgressed all the limits, the norms and laws, with his prophetic nature. The fact, that he has stood one alone against all, has been rendered his *jeweler's curse*.[1] He employs this extraordinarily apt and insightful expression in speaking about the hero of his novel, -- Cain Marchenoir. L. Bloy artistically and with genius has bestowed his curse upon the bourgeois world. In this he has been the modern sort of artist, and in this his artistry is amazing. With all his life he justifies the words of Ibsen's Doctor Stockmann ["An Enemy of the People"], in that the most mighty man is that one, who trods life's path, by himself alone.

The novel, "Le Désespéré", is the biography of a man of the Absolute, doomed to live in a bourgeois world of the relative and the conditional, and it is moreover an autobiography of L. Bloy himself, a description of his own desperation. And when one reads this novel, it becomes clear, that L. Bloy identifies his own anguished fate with the fate of Christ the Wretched, with the fate of the crucified Truth. A faith in God, not knowing qualms, doubts and waverings, becomes merged and identified with a faith in himself, in his own calling. He senses himself as in the very bosom of the Absolute, whereas he senses the bourgeois as an hater of everything of the Absolute. L. Bloy -- is a fanatic of the Absolute in life, and this fanaticism renders him ill-tempered and unrelenting towards people and the world. I tend to think, that in the Christianity of L. Bloy there are tendencies almost demonic, but there are also genuine elements of the seer, of things known only to him. He detected bourgeoisness throughout the whole of culture and could not live in it, he is filled with agony in cultural society. He sympathetically cites our Hertzen, terrified at European philistinism. He highly esteems Dostoevsky. His tense aestheticism does not soften him, it rather instead renders him all the more resolute; he experiences an ecstatic rapture of fanaticism, unbending, aloneness, the renegade, spite. God Himself -- assumes the guise of a poor and solitary sufferer. And L. Bloy wants likewise to be a poor and solitary sufferer, whereby from this position is sensed a Divine ecstasy. How he intends to combine his own individual religion of poverty, of aloneness, of the suffering of God with a Catholicism, such as desires a kingdom on earth and power over the world, remains his secret. This involved his

---

[1] *trans note*: apparently an idiomatic reference to various legends of pilfered jewels that bear a curse of harm.

religious drama. In the fate of Marchenoir, the hero of the "Le Désespéré" novel, it becomes possible to get a glimpse at all the tumult of spirit in L. Bloy himself, the moments of the God-struggling and resistance, and the moments of the God-submission and religious ecstasy. Marchenoir is living out a basic antinomy of Christianity: the promise of the kingdom and bliss, and the endlessly continuing of the torments of life. "When I beheld your friend so unhappy, it seemed to me, that I beheld God Himself in suffering upon the earth" ("Le Désespéré"). In these words of Veronica from "Le Désespéré" is the very heart of the matter in the religiosity of Bloy. Marchenoir says, that he is not a reactionary, that he is at the very forefront of progressives, "a pioneer to the very extent of the ultimate future" (Ibid.). This is very characteristic for Bloy. He tended to be regarded as a reactionary, a clericalist and royalist. He was perpetually singing the praises of the Middle Ages, he penned an apology of Marie Antoinette in 1896 under the intriguing title of "La Chevalière de la Mort" ("The Lady of Death"). But he is also a revolutionary, he is oriented towards the apocalyptic end. He prophesies about the catastrophic perishing of the bourgeois world, about the impending end. He sees in the anarchists a portent, an omen. The bourgeois will be too late to understand, what ought not to belong to it. Bloy -- is strong a revolutionary by temperament. He awaits the advent of the Paraclete. As a writer L. Bloy is not a shepherd, but instead a robber (as defined by Nietzsche). Each line, written by him, is a brigandage and revolution. His foresights become realised through indignation and spite. All more and more strongly there resound in him apocalyptic notes, the anticipation of the end and arrival of the new, the new spiriting breath of the Spirit. Every time, when one comes down into these catacombs, "there is the impression of being at the edge of the wellsprings, the edge of the whispering life of the forest, of the sunrises and sunsets in the meadows of Paradise, an impression at the very edge of the perception of the human soul" ("Pages choisies"). This is not the feelings of some mere aesthete, not a decadently sad feeling at the perishing of former beauty. This rather is a sense apocalyptic and prophetic. Marchenoir before his death says: "All my life I have wanted only two things: the Glory of God or death. Well, it is death that has come. And thus thanks for that. It is possible, that the glory will follow it and that my dilemma will have been for naught... I will now be judged, and not by the human sort judging. My wrathful writings, for which they so reproached me, will be weighed and compared against my natural talents and the deepest wishes of my heart. And one of these is -- I have endlessly desired justice, and I hope to receive the satisfaction, which has been promised us by Holy Scripture" ("Le Désespéré"). And L. Bloy anticipates the just judgement of God over the matter of his life. The monstrous injustice within human judgement stirs in him a resolute faith, that for him the judgement of God will be favourable.

"Le Désespéré" addresses the fate of a man. Marchenoir, pseudonym for L. Bloy himself, -- is a writer and a Catholic, impoverished and with disdain ignored by the bourgeois world. L. Bloy's other novel, "La Femme pauvre", addresses the fate of a woman. In it is sketched an image of feminine holiness and the attitude towards it by the bourgeois world. This is all again the selfsame fate of poverty in the world. The author does not promise some entertaining diversion, he promises the reverse. His novel is harsh and vexing. But in it there is depth, and it reveals the attitude of L. Bloy towards women. His attitude was that of an exceptionally masculine man and was not that of a soft and delicate cult of the feminine. In the religion of Bloy there is almost nothing of the cult of the Madonna, no consoling and recoursings to immersion in a Divine femininity. He did not seek to unburden his failings prayerfully before the Mother of God. All his religiousness was oriented towards Jesus Christ, Whom he sensed exclusively, and for Whom he had an exceptional love and experienced in his own particular paths in life. He is one of those, who totally takes to his heart the cross of crucifixion and seek therein something not easy and consoling, not some sweet sentimental emotions. His religion is of the masculine rough sort. Foreign to him is every tendency towards a religion with feminine aspects to the Divinity, which plays no small a role within Catholicism. But in his raving masculine soul, a different sort soul, not given to delicately soft sweetness, there lives the veneration of an image of womanly holiness, a veneration, totally cleansed and devoid of any sweet sentimentality, entirely chaste. He knows his wife and experienced a blindingly brilliant example of womanly integrity. And the image of Clotilde in "La Femme pauvre" is drawn with a masculine sort of tenderness, so rarely encountered, with a chaste passionateness. With L. Bloy there is a scathing disgust towards a "proper decent sort woman" ("femme honnête"), a boundless revulsion towards this "gueuse" ("vile creature"), as he terms her. "For a woman, a being as yet still temporarily held in lower a regard, there are only two essential images, two types, with which by necessity is to be reconciled the Infinitude, -- holiness and sensual voluptuousness. Between these two exists merely *the decent sort woman*, which is to say the bourgeois sort woman, absolutely abhorrent, who redeems no sort of sacrifice. The saint can fall low, and the fallen can rise up to the light, but neither of the two types become ever a decent sort woman, and when one such at Bethlehem refused hospitality to the Son of God, they are forever unable to escape their insignificance through some downfall or ascent" ("La Femme pauvre"). There is a vexing aspect to the veracity of the words of L. Bloy, that this "decent sort woman" having refused hospitality to the Saviour of the world, that her refusal was made out of a sense of bourgeois propriety, in the name of her own bourgeois domestic views. And therefore never does such a "decent woman" give shelter to the Poor Wretch, in hiding behind her bourgeois virtues. A fallen woman can give shelter to the Poor One, since she is moreso free and has in her the potential of an ascent to holiness. The image of Mary Magdalene was infinitely dear to L. Bloy, and he was filled with a pure and severe sympathy towards the prostitute. The "decent sort woman" is never with Christ the Poor -- she is always on the side of money and the world. L. Bloy: -- "Creation seems like a flower of the infinitely Poor One; and the utmost perfection of Whom they term the Almighty, was in this, that He was crucified, like a robber, in absolute disgrace" (Ibid.). Clotilde, who had nothing, who was completely poor, says: "I am quite happy, the entry into Paradise is not tomorrow, nor the day after, nor ten years after that, but the rather today, when a man is poor and crucified" (Ibid.). And Clotilde attains holiness though poverty. "Through suffering this living and strong Christian woman surmised, that there is only one way, particularly for women, to be in accord with God and that this path, quite singularly so, is with the Poor One. Not that facile, interesting and contrived sort of poverty, which is bestown charity by an hypocritical world, but rather a difficult poverty, shocking and scandalous, which needs help without any hope to glory and which can give nothing in return. She understood even, and this is nigh utmost, that a woman authentically exists only under this condition, that without the bread, the abode, friends, husband and children, and only by this can she manage to become aligned with the Saviour" (Ibid.). Suchlike a woman also was Clotilde -- an image, begotten of the reverential love of L. Bloy. This is both severely harsh and strange, and few would concur with Bloy on this. He tended to frighten everyone off from himself by his relentless radicalism. But these were not radical words of the cheap sort, but rather words, impelled by the power of the sacrificial blood, by which they were bought. Too few of us can repeat these words lightly. The French poverty of the XX Century is much more difficult, more complex and terrible, than it was in the XII Century, -- it is not so pretty, nor so emotionally moving. And those, who on an aesthetic level are enraptured with St. Francis, are turned off by L. Bloy. In him there is not the graced sense of the Franciscan love in the world and people; Bloy rather -- is a Christian, living the modern history, and in it has not remained vitally alive a place. L. Bloy however is lacking in freedom from the world and the world's evil, he is too filled with anger and indignation, he is too negatively dependent upon the evil. Foreign to him is the pervasively deep contemplation, meditation. His mystical life lacks concentration, is not disciplined. He is not an Apollonian in his spiritual life. The path of L. Bloy is so profoundly contrary to any sort of occult path. And in his path is to be sensed a quite individual calling. With an as yet unprecedented acuteness and radicalism he posits a dilemma for the Christian world, he demands a choice between Christ and the world. And thus his significance, perhaps, is greater than the significance of L. Tolstoy.

IV.

With L. Bloy there is no sort of an ideological system, no theory, no religio-philosophical teachings. His ideas are totally inseparable from his individual fate, from his intimate experiences. Everything that L. Bloy writes, is *something*, and not *about something*. He -- is, he exists. With L. Bloy there is a central idea of life, pervading every line written by him, and this idea is likewise his individual fate -- a theme of world history and his own individual theme. This -- is the theme regarding the Poor One and about money, this -- is the idea about the rift between Christ the Poor and the monied-world. The book, "Le Salut par les Juifs" ("Salvation is through the Jews") -- is one of the central works of L. Bloy. In it is lodged a quite exceptional, indeed unprecedented in its uniqueness, sense of Christ. In the strange dedication to this strange book, in which L. Bloy recounts, how to him as a poor man, some other poor fellow once anonymously sent twenty francs, and he straight off launches into proclaiming him self a messenger of the Absolute. This sense of being on a mission, of being sent, never quit him. For him, the theme about the Jews is a basic theme of world history. He religiously has a sense of Judaism and considers himself called to reveal the tragedy of Judaism, which is a tragedy involving all the world.

Nicholas Berdyaev

"Je ne suiset ne veut être ni dreyfusard, ni antidreyfusard, ni antisémite. Je suis anticochon, simplement, et, à ce titre, l'ennemi, le vomisseur de tout le monde, à peu près. Je suis, si on veut, l'homme... dont la main est levée contre tous et contre qui la main de tous est levée" ("Pages choisies").[1] He is contemptuous of anti-Semites on the order of Drumont [Édouard, 1844-1917]. And to him is repugnant the bourgeois attitude of these anti-Semites towards the Jews, with moreover the misunderstanding of the mysticism and metaphysics of Judaism.[2] L. Bloy is not able to belong to any sort of parties or currents, he has always stood alone. There is not one camp that could regard him as their own. He would be useful for none and dangerous for all. No sort of worldly advantage can be derived from recoursing to L. Bloy. And the vulgar anti-Semitism strives just the same to gain an advantage, as does Judaism, the bourgeois world just the same, as also does Judaism. In the profound religious sense of the words of L. Bloy, certainly, is an anti-Semite aspect. But his starting point is with an acknowledging of the Jews as the chosen people of God, through which salvation has come into the world. For him of absolute religious significance is this fact, that Christ was a Jew and could only be but a Jew. Christians often fail to sense this. The fate of Christianity cannot be separated from the fate of Judaism. In this is tied up the knot of the religious history of the world. "The Jews will be converted, if Jesus would come down from the Cross, and Jesus only thus would come down from the Cross, if the Jews would convert" ("Le Salut par les Juifs").[3] In what is

---

[1] "I am neither for Dreyfus, nor anti-dreyfus, nor an anti-Semite. I am anti the swinish, and simply stated, the enemy, the vomiter of all that world, little more. And I am, if you will, a man... whose hand is raised against all and against whom are raised the hands of all".

[2] The attitude of L. Bloy towards Judaism is very akin to my own, which I expressed in an article entitled "Nationalism and Anti-Semitism afront the Judgement of a Christian Consciousness" ("Russkaya mysl'", 1911 [*trans note*: actually the February 1912 issue, Kl. №168]. But I resolutely demand Christian an attitude towards Judaism.

[3] *trans note*: Cf. Mk. 15: 32 "*Let Christ the King of Israel now come down from the cross, wherefore we might see, and therefore believe*". The poignancy of this vexing and antinomic insight, and that it enters the Gospel narrative not fortuitously but intentionally, can be considered in

THE CRISIS OF ART

the meaning of this inescapable tragedy? "Jesus Christ was the ultimate authentic Poor Wretch -- singularly so amidst all the most poor, immeasurably more poor than any such as the Biblical Job, and as such the singular brilliant diamond and healing gemstone of the East of resplendent poverty, and was Himself the Poverty, proclaimed by the relentless pragmatic seers, whom the people pelted with stones. He had as companions three sorts of poverty, said a certain saint. He was poor in possessions, poor in friends, poor as regards His verymost Self. And this in the depth of the deeps, amidst the dank walls of a bottomless well" (Ibid.). The Jews "hated the Poor One with a boundless hatred". The Jews rendered Money separate from the Poor One. Christ -- is the Poor One, whereas the world -- is for Money. Through the Jews, hating and rejecting the Poor One, Christ became separated from the world, was crucified as regards the world. In this -- is the mystery of Golgotha. After Golgotha the aspect of Money became isolated from the Poor One, it began instead to lead an independent existence and gave birth to the bourgeois world. Herein is what comprises the mystery: "The death of Jesus essentially caused Money to become detached from the Poor One... The Universal Church, begotten of the Divine Blood, had its own designated aspect of the Poor One, but the Jews, reinforced in their impregnable fortress of obstinate despair, instead kept themselves the Money" (Ibid.). Money, riches, together with the Poor One, would have been in keeping with the Divine. The dividing away of money from the Poor One is also a separating away the world from the Divine Truth. This was like with a separating of the body from the soul. The dreadful thing about Money consists precisely in this, that "there is so little need of it, in order to gain one's way to the Second Person of the Trinity" (La femme pauvre"). L. Bloy sensed like no one else the secret and mystery of Money. He even wanted to write a book concerning Money, as a basic difficulty in life. In the Holy Scriptures, Money -- is synonymous with and symbolic of the living word of God. And yet what did the Jews do with such money? "They crucified it... they went

---

light of Jn. 20: 30-31, i.e. for a deliberate purpose (Why? Vide Jn. 20:31). Similarly, the historical lines of thought on the salvation of the Jews, suggested by St. Paul in Rom. 11: 26, 33, through the inscrutable ways of Divine Providence. How, and if so, it seems proper for God to decide, rather than trying to second-guess the Will of God, since "the devil is always in the details"...

about crucifying it, since this was a Jewish way of extirpating the Divine" ("Le Salut par les Juifs"). After this, Money fell away from its godly relationship, fell away into this world, became a matter of the godless kingdom of this world, instead of as formerly being symbolic of the Divine realm, of Divine might. And here L. Bloy in very unique and individual a form expresses the generally held Christian idea, that the Jews rejected Christ, because that they neither wanted nor could accept God manifest in a slave-like and lowly image, and they thus failed to recognise the Messiah in the guise of the Poor One. They would accept a Messiah powerful and glorious, establishing a kingdom of this world, a kingdom of the blessing of Israel. And this -- implies a rejection of the mystery of Golgotha, of the religious meaning of the Cross. In failing to understand the mystery of the Crucifixion, one thus crucifies. The world in following the Jews has not accepted the Crucified Christ and therefore continues to crucify Him. The Gospel history of Jesus Christ continues on still in the world. "The loathsome Judas continues on still to bestow his Judas-kiss to his Teacher in the garden, and Simon Peter all still ceases not the denying of Him, whilst huddling for warmth in the courtyard" (Ibid.). L. Bloy always sees Christ as crucified, remaining there not having come down from the Cross. Christ will come down from the Cross, when the Jews, when the world becomes converted to the Crucified One, when the aspect of Money is restored properly with the Poor One. It is possible to surmise, that L. Bloy confesses a religion of an eternal crucifixion, he accepts the Cross but without the hope of the Resurrection. He seems to have lost all earthly hopes and desires no sort of consolations. But he has his own consolation, which is when he looks backwards. He is not free of a romantic idealisation of the Middle Ages. And he all still cannot split off from ultimately his inherited religion, with his religion by-blood. Within this revolutionary lived still a romantic, having lost reactionary an hope. His fidelity to the Catholic Church is noble, and in it there is a tempting aestheticism. But was not the Catholic Church a sort of compromise with the issues of poverty and money, an adapting of Christ's truth to the world? In all his life and his every word, L. Bloy leads up to a setting of this question. But on a conscious level, for himself, he does not want to face this question, it offends his Latin aestheticism. Very distasteful for him is the spirit of Protestantism and its protest. He prefers to remain despondent, not knowing hopes as a Catholic, a Catholicism of which he understands for himself as a matter of crucifixion. In the Catholic life he has not yet seen

THE CRISIS OF ART

the Poor One and he has seen in it instead too much of the Money aspect, while strangely he himself took from Catholicism only the Poor One and rejected all the Money emphasis. His Catholic faith -- is deliriously tragic, having received nothing in recompense, except sweet ecstatic feelings of aloneness, non-acceptance and poverty.

V.

The "Exégèse des lieux communs" ("Explication of Commonplace Sayings") -- is a very fine fruition of the creative life of L. Bloy. This interpretation of the commonplace sayings of bourgeois wisdom are of genius in intent and the commonplaces, not everywhere uniform, are of genius in execution. All L. Bloy's discerning insights on bourgeoisness are condensed here and expressed with great acerbity. This book is striking by its metaphysical probity. It consists of smallish comments, a page or half in length, on various vital maxims of bourgeois wisdom, crystalised over the span of centuries. The selection of these sayings is amazing, and the list of headings along illustrates the quite exceptional sharpness of thought. And thus I shall offer some several of them:

"Dieu n'en demande pas tant" ("God demands only so much"). "Rien n'est absolu" ("Nothing is absolute"). "On n'est pafait" ("No one is perfect"). "Les affaires sont les affaires" ("The matter is what matters"; alt. "Doing it is what matters"). "Quand on est dans le commerce" ("Let it up to the merchants"). "Etre poète à ses heures" (Be a poet on your own time"). "Il faut hurler avec les loups" ("We have to howl with the wolves"; alt. "To live with wolves, one has to act the wolf"). "L'argent ne fait pas le bonheur, mais..." ("Happiness lies not in money, but still..."). "L'honneur des familles" ("The honour of families"). "Je pourrais être votre père" ("I'm old enough to be your father"). "Que voulez-vous, l'homme est l'homme" ("Well, what do you want, -- a man is only just a man"). "Assurer l'avenir de sas enfants" ("Secure a future for your children"). "Faire honneur à ses affaires" ("Be honourable in your doings"). "Perdre ses illusions" ("Lose your illusions"). "N'être pas le premier venu" ("Don't be at the head of the line"). "Faire un bon mariage" ("It's an advantage to get married"). "Si jeunesse savait, si vieillesse pouvait" ("If youth only knew, if old age only could"). "Chaque chose en son temps" ("Everything in its own time"). "Le bon Dieu" ("Good God"). "La santé avant tout" ("Best of all health"). "Dieu ne fait plus de miracles" ("God does not work miracles anymore").

Nicholas Berdyaev

Je ne suis pas plus bête qu'un autre" (I'm no more stupid/dumb than anyone else"). "Je ne veux pas mourir comme un chien" ("I don't want to die like a dog"). "L'honnête femme" ("A decent dame"). "Tout n'est pas rose dans la vie" ("Life is not always as rosy as it looks"). "Les belles années de l'enfance" ("The happy years of childhood"). "On..." ("They say..."). "Ce que la femme veut, Dieu le veut" ("Whatever a woman wants, is what God wants"), etc.

In France the bourgeoisness has attained classic a completion and perfection. Nowhere else is there such an extent of an aesthetically fashioned philistinism. Frances gives forth with the final fruits of the bourgeois culture. And thus in France there had to appear the greatest exposure of the bourgeoisness and a passionate hatred of the vile sort of bourgeois wisdom. The "Exégèse des lieux communs" -- is a mirror placed in front of the bourgeois world. In the radicalism and depth of his exposure of the boorish philistinism, L. Bloy stands higher than Ibsen. He penetrates into the very secrets of the stirrings of the bourgeois heart, of the bourgeois will and way of thinking, into the metaphysics of the bourgeois mystique. He exposes into the open the mystical roots of economic materialism. The bourgeoisness for L. Bloy is not a social category, as it is for the socialists, starting at but the surface level, nor is it even a psychological category, but rather instead a category metaphysical and mystical. The category of the *bourgeois* and *bourgeoisness* -- is fundamental in all his thinking and in all his views. He seeks to provide a metaphysics of the bourgeoisness, intuitively penetrating into the mystical depths of what comprises the bourgeois aspect. The scorn, anger, hate -- are methods of this intuitive approach, methods, yielding astonishing results. L. Bloy discerns, that every bourgeois person, even if he be a Christian and a good Catholic, believes only in this world, in the given, in necessity, in the useful in business and believes ultimately in naught else, nor in what has occurred consequent upon the Cross and Golgotha. "The resplendid rise of the bourgeois is grounded upon non-belief, even *after* he has seen and touched.[1] Yes, I say, -- and in spite of the impossibility of seeing and touching, with still non-belief as a consequence" ("Exégèse des lieux communs"). L. Bloy with genius gives a definition of idolatry: "Idolatry --

---

[1] *trans note*: the "*after*" is an allusion is to "doubting Thomas" -- Cf. Jn. 20: 24-29.

THE CRISIS OF ART

this is a preference of the seen over the unseen" ("Le mendiant ingrat"). The bourgeois is always an idolator, an idol-worshipper, since he likes as a slave to the seen. And how many such bourgeois idol-worshippers there are, even amongst the good Catholics! L. Bloy cannot bear the bourgeois sort of religiosity -- it is worse than atheism. With a blistering sarcasm he speaks on this, what *le bon Dieu* represents for the bourgeois: "Le bon Dieu du Bourgeois est une espèce de commis sont il n'est pas sûr et qu'il se garde bien d'honorer de sa confiance... il n'y a pas à dire, le bon Dieu est extrêmement décoratif dans les boutiques. On sait cela, quand on est dans le commerce... Je ne serais pas étonné si, quelque jour, un huissier de grande banlieue me faisait présenter un commandement par le bon Dieu parlant à ma personne"[1] ("Exégèse..."). The bourgeois appeared in the world, when Money became separated from the Poor One, and the world in turn became cut off from Christ. The bourgeois aspect involves also "the world". The bourgeois aspect has crucified Christ anew and continues eternally to crucify Him. "Now the bourgeois has a substitute in place of Christ" (Ibid.). For the bourgeois "work -- is his God, his Absolute". "Etre dans les affaires, c'est être dans l'Absolu" ("To be concerned with one's own affairs is a being in touch with the Absolute") (Ibid.). "Work -- is work, just as God -- is God. This is a distinction foremost of all. One's work, one's affairs -- becomes something inexplicable, mysterious, imperishable" (Ibid.). And L. Bloy hates everything to do with "business", refuses to accept the mystique of "business". The bourgeois has many of his own secrets, altogether undetectable from the outside. There exist mysteries of bourgeoisness, towards which one mustneeds become attuned, in order to grasp them. For L. Bloy, the entirety of bourgeois economics is a theology, a reverse sort of theology; the bourgeois wisdom -- is a sort of inside-out or upside-down rehash of the Divine wisdom. "Never has a Mexican or Papuan New Guinea idol been so adored, as the bourgeois adores himself, nor demanded such terrible human sacrifices" (Ibid.). "By

---

[1] "The good God for the Bourgeois is something on the order of the sales-clerk, whom one does not quite trust nor do the honour of taking into one's confidence... It is impossible to deny, that the good God is extremely adept at decorating the boutiques. This goes without saying, for anyone involved in commerce... I would not be surprised, if sometime ahead, some bailiff from the grand suburbs should present me a commandment on behalf of the good God, addressed to me personally".

his nature the bourgeois -- is an hater and destroyer of Paradise. When he takes notice of some beautiful spot, his dream -- is to cut down the trees, dry up the streams, to lay out roads, open up shopping and... He calls this a "monter une affaire" ("starting the matter") (Ibid.). And thus the bourgeois tends to express his mysteries: "Faire travailler l'argent" ("Money ought to show a profit"); "Il faut mourir riche" ("One should die rich"); "Quand on est dans le commerce" ("To be business-minded"); "Etre pratique" ("To be practical"); "Rentrer dans son argent" ("To get a return on one's money"); "Assurer l'avenir à ses enfants" ("To assure the future of one's children"); "Le temps c'est l'argent" ("Time is money"), and so on, and so on... "The grandiose fate of the bourgeois is a sort of upside-down redemption, as Christians might tend to comprehend it. For him alone the human race has to be crucified. It was necessary, Christians say, that the Son of God be incarnated, suffer under Pontius Pilate and die on the Cross, so that all people thereby might be redeemed. But here it is the opposite. It was inevitable, necessary, absolutely and forever, that every being, either voluntary or involuntary, should be offered in sacrifice, so that the bourgeois can go about his digestion calmly, with his gut and kidneys safe and secure, whilst knowing, that he is a genuine god and that all has been wrought just for him" ("Exégèse..."). But there will be a day, when Christ will say to the bourgeois: "I am -- the Money Itself, and I know thee not" (Ibid.).

The basis for the bourgeois wisdom -- consists in the commonplace saying, "Dieu n'en demande pas taut" ("God demands only so much"), and it is with this that L. Bloy begins his exegetical investigation. The bourgeois as it were bargains with God. When the bourgeois says, that God demands only so much, then this merely means, that "*He Himself [the self-worshipping bourgeois]* demands only so much ("Exégèse..."). "Once God demands only just so much, then as an inevitable consequence of this, He is compelled to demand all less and less and in the final end to altogether refuse demanding". This wise bourgeois maxim secures himself the possibility to give as little as possible. The same sort of bourgeois wisdom is expressed also in the maxims: "Rien n'est absolu" ("Nothing is absolutely so"); "On n'est pas parfait" ("No one is perfect"); "Je ne suis pas un saint" ("I am no saint"); "Que voulez-vous! L'homme est l'homme" ("What do you expect! A man is only just a man"), and many others. These clichés of bourgeois wisdom L. Bloy opposes with his own religious maximalism. With L. Bloy, there is the idea of a radical departure from the world, of a revolutionary breaking away from the bourgeois aspect. He lives in the world like an holy fool -- inwardly he is a gone man. But this is a different sort departure, than that of the peculiar departure effected by Aleksandr Dobroliubov [1876-1945]. L. Bloy puts up totally with the humiliation and the scorn. He thinks, that a Christian ought to live by charity and ought not to strive towards some new arrangement for life, such as Lev Tolstoy intended. He consciously did not want and cannot occupy himself in the bread profession, such as the bourgeois world might demand of him and his hero Marchenoir. L. Bloy does not allow for any sort of compromise of Christianity with the bourgeois world. The Christian life for him -- is a crazy, suffering, disordered life. And only such a life -- is absolute. Foreign to him is the ideal of a balanced and harmonised Christian life. To him is foreign even a balanced and orderly holiness. God demands infinitely much, all the moreso. "I am among those, who would wish, that a revolution should spread about and that the intolerable tyranny of the bourgeoise -- the old enemy of adventure -- be countered by the modern agitations of the bourgeois-ruffians, who do not want to hear anything more about any limits. This catastrophe would be of some comfort to our planet" (Ibid.).

      The "Exégèse des lieux communs" -- is a book, replete with incisive and acerbic definitions and judgements, some profound, others frivolous in the spirit of the French genius. Hence such characteristic places: "A microbe with a delay of some sixty centuries after the creation of the world has emerged finally from nothingness. What a revolution! With its arrival, everything changes. The searchings for the tiny critter serves as a replacement for the old spirit of the Crusades". "The divine science has reached down so low, that even a bourgeois sort can grasp it". Which is to say that science -- a Divine knowledge -- becomes adapted to bourgeois interests. "Just try to imagine getting someone of importance started on renewing the Fourth Crusade". We already know, that one of the most bitter feelings in L. Bloy -- was his hatred towards a "decent sort woman", that eternally notorious bourgeois woman in Bethlehem, who at the inn turned away the Infant-Saviour. "L'honnête femme est la morose et brûlante épouse du grand Cocu déchaîné... O prostituées sans mensonge pour qui Jésus a souffert, pitoyables et saintes putains qui n'avez pas honte des pauvres et qui témoignerez au Dernier jour, que pensez-vous de cette gueuse?"[1] "Etre dans les nuages" ("To be up in the clouds") -- is something the bourgeois disapproves of and ridicules. "What a vexing episode the Ascension [of Christ to Heaven] must seem to the bourgeois, and how shocked he ought to be at Jesus, rising off up into the sky! God is gone off up into the clouds!... And indeed who could be finer a Christian, than the bourgeois sort? Who, if not he, that announces all the philanthropic initiatives in our parishes...".

The caustic and individual uniqueness of language with L. Bloy gets rather lost in the translation and is almost unrenderable, in trying to convey the nuances from the French. "Si je vois une bourgeoise enceinte, il m'est impossible de ne pas penser à la naissance prochaine d'un petit et j'avoue que cela me parait plutôt troublant. Je ne vois même pas très bien en quoi la famille peut y être intéressée, sinon dans le sens le plus fâcheux. Car enfin le Bourgeois n'est pas patriarche et ne doit pas l'être. Les vertus patriarchales sont juste le contraire des vertus dont il s'honore... Même lorsqu'il engendre, le Bourgeois est dans les affaires".[2] "Autrefois, il y a cinquante ans à peine, la nuit, ou si on veut, les ténèbres du Moyen Age étaient rigoureusement exigées dans les examens. Un jeune bourgeois qui aurait douté de l'opacité de ces ténèbres n'aurait pas trouvé à se marier".[3]

---

[1] "This decent sort woman is the morose and irritable spouse of some sop of a grand lout... O ye prostitutes without hypocrisy for whom Jesus suffered; ye pitiful and saintly harlots, who are not ashamed of the poor and who will testify on the day of Judgement, -- what do you think of this vile woman?"

[2] "If I see some bourgeois that is pregnant, it becomes impossible for me not to think about the birth of the petit bourgeois and I avow that it seems rather troubling. I do not see very well even in what the family can be interested, albeit in more regrettable a sense. Because ultimately the bourgeois cannot be of the patriarch sort and has a duty not to be so. The patriarchal sorts of virtue are just the opposite to the virtues that he holds dear... Even when he begets, the bourgeois is all about business".

[3] "Upon a time, even fifty years back, the so-called night, or if you will the darkness of the Middle Ages was rigorously required in examinations. A young bourgeois who displayed doubts on the opacity of this darkness would likely have had dim hopes of finding a wife.

THE CRISIS OF ART

"Dieu ne fait plus de miracles" -- "c'est une manière conciliante, bénigne, quasipieuse, de dire qu'il n'en a jamais fait...".[1] When the bourgeois sort say, that they do not understand Barbey d'Aurevilly, Villiers de l'Isle-Adam, E. Hello, Verlaine, he yet further adds: " -- "Cependent nous ne sommes pas plus bêtes que d'autres." Et à l'instant, Verlaine, Hello, Villiers, Barbey et même, si vous voulez, Napoléon et tous les grands personnages seront aperçus sous leurs pieds... L'universelle supériorité de l'homme qui n'est pas plus bête qu'un autre est ce que je connais de plus écrasant".[2] The bourgeois sort love to say: " -- "Je ne veux pas mourir comme un chien". Il est permis a demander, pourquoi un homme qui a vecu comme un cochon a le désir de ne pas mourir comme un chien".[3] "Quand le bourgeois vous dit qu'il est philosophe, cela signifie tout simplement qu'il a le ventre plein, la digestion sans embargo, le pote-monnaieou le du le porte-feuille convenablement dodu et que, par conséquent, il se fout du reste "comme de l'An quarante".[4] "They say", -- in this nuance is likewise summed up the bourgeois wisdom. "Chaque fois que le bourgeois parle, ce mystérieux "on" sonne comme un sac d'argent posé lourdement à terre,

---

[1] "God no longer works miracles" -- "this is a conciliatory, benign, semi-pious way of saying that He never did...".

[2] " -- "But we are no more stupid than others". And this at a moment when Verlaine, Hello, Villiers, Barbey, and even if you will Napoléon and all the great personages get trampled underfoot... The universal superiority of the man who is no more stupid than another is what I consider the most dismaying".

[3] " -- "I don't want to die like a dog". If one be permitted to ask, why should a man that has lived like a swine, not desire to die like a dog".

[4] "When the bourgeois tells you he is a philosopher, this signifies simply that he has a full belly, his digestion suffering no embargo, his wallet or billfold is conveniently plump, wherefore he does not care in the least "about what happened back in the decade of the forties"".

dans une chambre voisine, où quelqu'un aurait été assassiné".[1] There is a great bit of beauty in the concluding epilogue to this investigation of commonplace sayings. "Que ferez-vous, quand on vous mettra en croix? Demande quelqu'un. -- Moi, je ferai de beaux rêves, réspond ma petit Madeleine âgée de cinq ans".[2] In these touching and powerful words there shines through in life for L. Bloy -- beautiful dreams of one crucified on a cross. And thus is his reply to the bourgeois world, such as has crucified truth and beauty.

VI.

Already up in age, L. Bloy wrote his book, "L'Âme de Napoléon" ("The Soul of Napoléon"), which can be considered one of his most remarkable writings. Within it are coalesced apocalyptic views, a feeling of the impending end and presentiments of what is to come. In the book dedication he says, "There is ensuing the evening of world life, my dear child, and thou perhaps will be a witness to Divine and to terrible things, the majestic foretype of which would be in a victorious emperor". L. Bloy from his childhood was into the cult of Napoléon. Here is how he describes his attitude towards Napoléon at the age of twelve: "In everything he seemed to me to be omnipotent and faultless, like God Himself, and I in my imagination fancied myself a veteran of his old guard.

And what further was there for me to understand? I already felt and never ceased to feel a supernatural strength in him and even at present I am looking at the eight blood-red letters, comprising his name, boldly set upon the book cover, and they are as it were luminous with rays of light, reaching to the farthest ends of the universe" ("L'Âme de Napoléon"). He writes in a diary: "I am intent upon finishing my booklet on the life of Napoléon. This great man for me was so steeped in blood, that I cannot hear of him in cool a manner" ("Pages choisies"). And like always, he

---

[1] "Every time the bourgeois speaks, this mysterious "they say" sounds like an heavy sack of money there on the ground, or in some adjoining chamber, where there might be an assassin lurking".

[2] "What will you do when you are put on the cross?? -- asks someone. Me, I will make beautiful dreams, -- answers my little Madeleine, age five".

begins to identify his own fate with the fate of Napoléon: "I have my own legend, just like with Napoléon and certain criminals". The cult of Napoléon is the cult of a man solitary and misunderstood. "He was a loner, boundlessly and terribly a loner, and upon this aloneness lay the seal of eternity... Napoléon, like some prehistoric monster that somehow survived after the disappearance of its kind, was completely alone, he did not have companions capable of understanding and supporting him, he had no visions of angels, and possibly, he did not even believe in God, who's to know?" ("L'Âme de Napoléon"). And L. Bloy concludes this chapter of his book with the incisive and powerful words, penetrating at depth into the secret of the solitary aloneness: "Il fuit seul enfin surtout au milieu de lui-même, oùil errait tel qu'un lépreux inabordable dans un palais immense et désert. Seul â jamais, comme la Montagne ou l'Océan!"[1] Here, as always, the aloneness seems for him Divine an aspect and evokes in him fond reverence. Beautifully spun together in his head is the aloneness of L. Bloy himself, the aloneness of Napoléon, the aloneness of God. Napoléon was a profoundly unhappy man. Happiness is impossible for a great man. The happiness of earthly life -- is all but the ephemeral content of satisfied needs, which "be not of consequence to a great man and moreover the greatest of people". Whoever has never been impoverished can but understand nothing in the history of Napoléon. "Il fuit, au seuil de sun âme, le Mendiant de l'Infini, le Mendiant toujours anxieux de sa propre fin, qu'il ignorait, qu'il ne pouvait pas compredre; le Mendiant extraordinaire et colossal demandant â qui passait le petit sou de l'empire du monde, la faveur insigne de contempler en lui-même le Paradis terrestre de sa propre gloire et qui mourut, au bout de la terre, les mains vides et le coeur brisé, avec les poids de plusieurs millions d'agonies!"[2] How

---

[1] "But nowhere was he so alone, as but with himself, wandering like a leper through his immense and deserted palace. Eternally alone, like a mountain or the ocean!"

[2] "He was, at the threshhold of his soul, the Indigent Beggar of Infinitude, an Indigent always anxious over his own proper end, of which he was ignorant, nor could understand; the extraordinary and colossal Indigent Beggar who demanded as the paltry coin the empire of the world, the favour to contemplate in himself the earthly paradise of his own glory and who died at an extremity of the earth, empty-handed and with broken heart, bearing the burden of some millions of agonies!"

passionate the fondness, that has for the object of his love in all that he loves, by which he is captivated -- the aloneness, the lack of acceptance, the poverty. And it seems to him, that God Himself loves Napoléon with exceptional a love. "Dieu a regardé dans le sang liquide des carnages et ce miroir lui a renvoyé la face de Napoléon, il l'aime comme sa propre image; il chérit ce Violent comme il chérit ses Apôtres, ses Martyrs, ses Confesseurs le plus doux; il le caresse tendrement des ses puissantes mains tel qu'un maître impérieux carressant une vierge farouche qui refuserait de se dévêtir".[1] And L. Bloy ventures a bold definition of Napoléon: "Napoléon -- is the visage of God within time". How is a Christian to understand these strange words? In Napoléon was a Divine force, but refracted within the darkness, acting in the dark. L. Bloy grants, as do many mystics, that in God there is also a darkly obscure visage and that in this darkly obscure visage it is possible to reverence a Divine force. The daydream about a superman and a supra-human power lived within the soul of L. Bloy, it was there daily with his impassioned cult of the great and heroic. He investigates Napoléon in apocalyptic a manner. "I do not think, that throughout all his life there was scarcely a single action or circumstance, which would be possible not to interpret as providential, as a foretokening of the Kingdom of God on earth". The decretal concerning a continental blockade L. Bloy terms as "apocalyptic". "An apocalyptic decree, as though on the eve of the Dread Last Judgement!" "Napoléon -- the Emperor in capital letters and for all time". And Bloy exclaims: "Without my Emperor I cannot conceive of Paradise". He was sent, "in order *by the hands of the Gallic people to carry out the intent of God*, to remind all the peoples of the earth about the existence of God"; "God intended Napoléon, just as He intended all the Popes, just as He intended His Church". What indeed was Napoléon? "Napoléon is incomprehensible, and unconditionally so, he was the most enigmatic man in the world, since he, first and foremost of all, -- is a foretype of He Who

---

[1] "God hath gazed upon this bloody carnage and its mirror reflects back the face of Napoléon, whom He doth love as in His Own Image; He doth cherish this violent one just as He doth cherish His Apostles, His Martyrs, His moreso meek Confessors; He caresses him with His powerful hands as might an imperious master caress a timid virgin hesitant to disrobe".

THE CRISIS OF ART

has to come again into the world and Who, perhaps, is already nigh close; Napoléon -- is His foretype and fore-runner amongst us, and His coming is prepared for by all the eminent predecessors". Who is it, that has to come? This is not yet the Christ of the Second Coming nor is it the Anti-Christ, this rather indeed is the Man -- a superman, the foretype of which has been everything great. With L. Bloy there is a real sort apocalyptic self-feeling, but he romantically connects it with the cult of Napoléon. He confesses a French messianism, akin to the Polish and Russian messianism, the messianism of the Slavophils, of Dostoevsky, of Vl. Solov'ev. The phenomenon of Napoléon, singular within world history as to his power and extraordinary aspect, tends to reinforce the feel of French messianism. "France -- is the living soul of all the peoples". "Only God can heal France". "When she [France] suffers, God Himself suffers, the awesome God doth agonise on account of all the earth, issuing forth with blood". Thus he wrote in a preface to a book about war of 1870, "Sueur de Sang" ("Bloody sweat"). "If France be accursed in having spurned God, and lain prostrate underfoot of peoples, if this mustneeds be expected, then let it perish and let it all end, and let our planet, having lost its soul, let it plunge like a dead thing into the Infinitude" ("Pages choisies"). Without France, Bloy cannot conceive himself as alive in the world. "When however will that one appear, whose arrival has been anticipated by the worldwide upheaval of peoples under Napoléon? He, undoubtedly, will come unto France... He will come in the name of God or against God -- of this we do not know. But it is indisputable, that this will be a man, of whom to expect either evil or good things, -- an heavenly messenger of joy or of despair, whose arrival was proclaimed by the prophets, about whom noised forth beasts both the timid and the fierce, and joyously or despondently the birds did sing..." ("L'Âme de Napoléon"). This man will be the crown of creation, its ultimate end. The actual man has not yet been born. L. Bloy believes, that the French -- are the chosen people of God and that in France will be realised the messianic expectations. And yet he senses the dissolution and ruination of France, the victory of the realm of bourgeoisness. There is a great depth in this uncertainty, whether the anticipated man will come on behalf of God or against God. And in this is a sensing of the ultimate freedom of man. This apocalyptic anticipation -- for L. Bloy is very mysterious and very audacious. Napoléon wanted to act as though the hand of Providence! "Indeed as of Providence! In these words consists all the entirety of Napoléon. Dimly he sensed himself called to be the predecessor of that one, who would renew the face of the earth, and he imagined, that he himself was destined for this role, and many shared in this mistake. Therefore over the course of ten years he was successful as the supreme arbiter, shaping and fashioning Europe in accord with his taste". In L. Bloy there is as it were a blurred double image regarding Christ and the Anti-Christ. In L. Bloy's understanding, the destiny of Man includes within it something totally irrational and antinomic. No one single man on earth knows his own true destiny. "No one knows his own destiny in this world, nor to what his actions, his feelings, his thoughts will lead to; who will be the closest of all to him among people and what will be his true name, his imperishable name, inscribed in the Book of Light. Neither an emperor, nor a simple stevedore knows truly his burden, nor his crown". A fundamental problem throughout all the life of L. Bloy has been the problem of individual fate. And he always sensed within this fate a transpiring of the Apocalypse. The fate of Napoléon is the apocalyptic fate of Man at its summit, the foretype of the fate of the superman, a combination of might with aloneness, of the regal with the indigent. Bloy perceives within Napoléon a great poet of life: "It is impossible to understand Napoléon, without glimpsing in him the poet, an incomparable poet in action. His verses -- all this is his life, having no equal. He always thought and acted like a poet, for whom all the visible world is no more than a mirage". The book of L. Bloy on Napoléon -- is likewise a poem, in which he lodged his beautiful dreams, dreams of the crucified, the indigent and the alone. And in this dreams -- is greater a truth, than in the visible actuality, since poetry is more real, more of essence than prose.

VII.

Léon Bloy -- is a phenomenon quite individual and unrepeatable. He does not teach some pathway, and it is impossible to be a follower of his. He -- is a completed sort of aesthetic phenomenon. But everything written by L. Bloy is imbued with a rare quality of vital conviction. And yet the difficult life of L. Bloy, and the blood of his heart serves to prove his truth better and more powerfully than all the indicated thoughts. L. Bloy -- is a writer in the lofty sense of the word, which is alien to the bourgeois world and the bourgeois age, a writer thus of fading a type. His writing was for him a matter of service and it emerged from all the ramifications of a differentiated culture. L. Bloy -- is on the order of the Jew, and not the Hellene (i.e. the Greek). He devoted all to the One Only, all flowed together into a single passion and a single impulse. He had no desire to know multiplicity in the world. This renders him difficult, tedious and for many quite distasteful. In him there is something aggressive, compulsive. He sets poverty higher than love. But how distinctly different is his Latin exaltation of poverty from the Slavic exaltation of poverty. Russians love poverty differently, from how L. Bloy loves it. With L. Bloy there is thus the feel of a Latin cult of strength and power. Impoverished, alone and rejected -- he knows regal sort an experience of this. He is intimately close to the heart of the indigent poor. He loves the poor man, loves him more, than L. Tolstoy does. But somewhere at depth he loves riches -- wealth, but not the rich, he loves it as a Latin, an aesthete and the herald of a lordly, not slave-like morals. In him, there is not the phony unctuousness, none of that fake humility, which so readily passes over into boorish hamism. An enormous objective service of L. Bloy -- is in the revealing of the theological basis to economics, an exposure on the metaphysics of money. But his even greater merit consists in this, in that he has had the audacity right through to the end to be himself, in his writings to be a man, totally open.[1] His brigand sort manner of life and robber sort roughness in writing are more instructive, than a pastoral manner of life and lyrical manner of writing. He -- is a great moralist without the moralism. And foremost of all he teaches a boundless bravery in facing the terrors of life. This bravery is something great, and a singular attainment of religious experience. The religious experience of L. Bloy flows beyond the borders of Catholicism, just as also it does beyond every static religious form. Striking is his prayer of the poor man, with which he concludes his wrathful book, "Les dernières colonnes de l'Eglise" ("The Final Pillars of the Church"). "Lord Jesus! I would prefer, that Thou had no home. Look upon these pillars of the Church, which do provide no possibility from afar to catch sight of Thee upon Thine altar. True, I am quite brazen, in speaking to Thee thus, since I am a sinner and hardly dare to lift my eyes. True it is likewise, that I am bare-footed and have neither wallet, nor money-purse. But did Thou not similarly send forth Thy

---

[1] *trans note*: this is reminiscent of the description of Nathanael by Jesus (Jn. 1:47) as "*an Israelite without guile*"...

disciples,[1] mysteriously counselling them to bow before no one along the journey. Thou justly shalt reward me, that I have bowed before no one over the long while of my wanderings amongst people, as one in desperation, having become companion of the eternal Wanderer. And I cry out to Thee, O Lord. Is it possible, that Thou dwellest still in the habitation, which these misfits term Thine and which they seek to prop up as unshakable pillars? Thou goest along the roads and the fields,[2] Thou shalt live on within the ardent and trembling hearts of the few beaten with stones, who will be Thine poor ones and to whom Thou wouldst bestow Thine dominion. Nigh close is the hour of the coming of the Paraclete, and no one ever will have seen anything more beautiful!" And it is thus that L. Bloy surmounts the tragedy of the Latin spirit and religiously emerges upon the vista of roads and fields.

---

[1] *trans note*: Cf. Lk. 10: 1-4ff.

[2] *trans note*: cf. Mt. 8:19-20: "*Et accedens unus scriba, ait illi: Magister, sequar te, quocumque ieris. Et dicit ei Iesus: volpes foveas habent, et volucres caeli nidos: filius autem hominis non habet ubi caput reclinet*".
"*And a certain scholar came unto Him saying: Master, I shalt follow Thee, whithersoever Thou goest. And Jesus saieth unto him: the foxes have their dens and the birds of the air their nests, but the Son of Man hath nowhere to recline His head*"...

Threefold Triadic Hierarchy of Angelic Ranks

08 NOVEMBER (XI - 21)

The Sobor (Assemblage) of the Chief of the Heavenly Hosts Michael and the Other Heavenly Bodiless Powers. The Archangels: Gabriel, Raphael, Uriel, Selaphiel, Jehudiel, Barachiel, and Jeremiel. Nun Martha of Pskov.

The Celebration of the Sobor (Assemblage) of the Leader of the Heavenly Hosts Michael, and the Other Heavenly Bodiless Hosts was established at the beginning of the IV Century at the local Laodician Council, which occurred several years subsequent to the First OEcumenical Council. The Laodician Council by its 35th Canon condemned and renounced as heretical the worship of angels as creators and rulers of the world and it affirmed their proper Orthodox veneration. A feastday was established in November -- the ninth month from March (with which month the year began in ancient times) -- in accordance with the 9 Ranks of Angels. The eighth day of the month was decreed for the intended Sobor (Assemblage) of all the Heavenly Powers -- in conjunction with the Day of the Dread Last-Judgement of God, which the holy fathers called the "Eighth Day", -- since after this age in which the seven days [of Creation] have elapsed will come the "Eighth Day", -- and then there "shalt come the Son of Man in His Glory and all the holy Angels together with Him" (Mt. 25: 31).

The Angelic Ranks are divided into three Hierarchies: -- highest, middle, and lowest. In the Highest Hierarchy are included the three Ranks: the Seraphim, Cherubim and Thrones. Closest of all to the MostHoly Trinity stand the six-winged **Seraphim** [Seraphimy] (Flaming, and Fiery) (Is. 6: 12). They blaze with love for God and impel others to it.

After the Seraphim there stand before the Lord the many-eyed **Cherubim** [Cheruvimy] (Gen. 3: 24). Their name means: outpouring of wisdom, enlightenment, since through them, -- radiating with the light of Divine-knowledge and understanding of the mysteries of God, there is sent down wisdom and enlightenment for true Divine-knowledge.

After the Cherubim -- stand God-bearing through grace given them for their service, the **Thrones** [Prestoly] (Col. 1: 16), mysteriously and incomprehensibly upholding God. They serve the uprightness of God's justice.

Nicholas Berdyaev

The Middle Angelic Hierarchy consists of three Ranks: Dominions, Powers, and Authorities.

Dominions [Gospodstva] (Col. 1: 16) hold dominion over the successive ranks of Angels. They instruct the earthly authorities, established from God, to wise governance. The Dominions influence rule by miracles, they quell sinful impulses, subordinate the flesh to the spirit, and provide mastery over the will to conquer temptation.

Powers [Sily] (1 Pet. 3: 22) fulfill the will of God. They work the miracles and send down the grace of wonderworking and perspicacity to saints pleasing to God. The Powers give assist to people in bearing obediences, encourage them in patience, and give them spiritual strength and fortitude.

Authorities [Vlasti] (1 Pet. 3: 22, Col. 1: 16) have authority to quell the power of the devil. They repel from people demonic temptations, uphold ascetics and guard them, helping people in the struggle with evil ponderings.

In the Lowest Hierarchy are included the three Ranks: Principalities, Archangels, and Angels.

Principalities [Nachala] (Col. 1: 16) have command over the lower angels, instructing them in the fulfilling of Divine commands. To them are entrusted to direct the universe, and protect lands, nations and peoples. Principalities instruct people to render honour to everyone, as becomes their station. They teach those in authority to fulfill their necessary obligations, not for personal glory and gain, but out of respect for God and benefit for neighbour.

Archangels [Arkhangely] (1 Thess. 4: 16) announce about the great and most holy, they reveal the mysteries of the faith, prophecy and understanding of the will of God, they intensify deep faith in people, enlightening their minds with the light of the Holy Gospel.

Angels [Angely] (1 Pet. 3: 22)are closest to all to people. They proclaim the intent of God, guiding people to virtuous and holy life. They protect believers restraining them from falling, and they raise up the fallen; never do they abandon us and always they are prepared to help us, if we so desire.

All the Ranks of the Heavenly Powers have in common the name Angels -- by virtue of their service. The Lord reveals His will to the highest of the Angels, and they in turn inform the others.

THE CRISIS OF ART

Over all the Nine Ranks, the Lord put the Holy Leader ("Archistrategos") Michael (his name in translation from the Hebrew means -- "who is like unto God") -- a faithful servitor of God, wherein he hurled down from Heaven the arrogantly proud day star Lucifer together with the other fallen spirits. And to the remaining Angelic powers he cried out: "Let us attend! Let us stand aright before our Creator and not ponder that which is displeasing unto God!" According to Church tradition, in the church service to the Archistrategos Michael concerning him, he participated in many other Old Testament events. During the time of the Exodus of the Israelites from Egypt he went before them in the form of a pillar of cloud by day and a pillar of fire by night. Through him the power of the Lord was made manifest, annihilating the Egyptians and Pharaoh who were in pursuit of the Israelites. The Archangel Michael defended Israel in all its misfortunes.

He appeared to Jesus Son of Navin (Joshua) and revealed the will of the Lord at the taking of Jericho (Nav. / Josh. 5: 13-16). The power of the great Archistrategos of God was manifest in the annihilation of the 185 thousand soldiers of the Assyrian emperor Sennacherib (4 [2] Kings 19: 35); also in the smiting of the impious leader Antiochos Illiodoros; and in the protecting from fire of the Three Holy Youths -- Ananias, Azarias and Misail, thrown into the fiery furnace for their refusal to worship an idol (Dan. 3: 22 25).

Through the will of God, the Archistrategos Michael transported the Prophet Avvakum (Habbakuk) from Judea to Babylon, so as to give food to Daniel, locked up in a lions' den (Kondak of Akathist, 8).

The Archangel Michael prevented the devil from displaying the body of the holy Prophet Moses to the Jews for idolisation (Jude 1: 9).

The holy Archangel Michael showed his power when he miraculously saved a lad, cast by robbers into the sea with a stone about his neck at the shores of Athos (Athos Paterikon).

From ancient times the Archangel Michael was famed by his miracles in Rus'. In the Volokolamsk Paterikon there is included a narrative of the Monk Paphnutii of Borovsk with an account of Tatar "baskaki" (tax-gatherers) concerning the miraculous saving of Novgorod the Great: "And wherefore Great Novgorod never was taken by the Hagarites... when by the sufferance of God for our sins the godless Hagarite emperor Batu devoured and set aflame the Russian land and was come to the New City (i.e. Novgorod) and God and the MostHoly Mother of God shielded it with an appearance of Michael the Archistrategos, which did forbid him to enter into it. He [Batu] was come to the Lithuanian city and did come towards Kiev and did see the stone church over the doors of which the great Archangel Michael had written and spoken unto the prince his allotted fate: 'By this we have forbidden entry into Great Novgorod'".

Intercession for Russian cities by the MostHoly Queen of Heaven always involved Her appearances with the Heavenly Hosts, under the leadership of the Archistrategos. Grateful Rus' acclaimed the MostPure Mother of God and the Archangel Michael in church singing. To the Archistrategos Michael are dedicated many a monastery, cathedrals, court and merchant churches. In old Kiev at the time of the accepting of Christianity, there was erected a cathedral of the Archangel, and a monastery also was built in his name. Archangel cathedrals stand at Smolensk, Nizhni Novgorod, Staritsa, a monastery at Great Ustiug (beginning XIII Century), and a cathedral at Sviyazhsk. In Rus' there was not a city, wherein was not a church or chapel, dedicated to the Archangel Michael. One of the chief temples of the city of Moscow -- the burial church in the Kremlin -- is dedicated to him. Numerous and beautiful icons of the Chief-in-Rank of the Highest Powers are also in his Cathedral. One of these -- the Icon "Blest Soldiery" --written in the Uspenie (Dormition) Cathedral of the Moscow Kremlin, where the saintly soldiers -- Russian princes -- are depicted under the leadership of the Archistrategos Michael.

From Sacred Scripture and Sacred Tradition are likewise known the Archangels: **Gabriel** -- strength (power) of God, herald and servitor of Divine almightiness (Dan. 8: 16, Lk. 1: 26); **Raphael** -- the healing of God, the curer of human infirmities (Tobit 3: 16, 12: 15); **Uriel** -- the fire or light of God, enlightener (3 Ezdras 5: 20); **Selaphiel** -- the prayer of God, impelling to prayer (3 Ezdras 5: 16); **Jehudiel** -- the glorifying of God, encouraging exertion for the glory of the Lord and interceding about the reward of efforts; **Barachiel** -- distributor of the blessing of God for good deeds, entreating the mercy of God for people; **Jeremiel** -- the raising up to God (3 Ezdras 4:36).

On icons the Archangels are depicted in accord with the trait of their service:

Michael -- tramples the devil underfoot, and in his left hand holds a green date-tree branch, and in his right hand -- a spear with a white banner (or sometimes a fiery sword), on which is outlined a scarlet cross.

THE CRISIS OF ART

Gabriel -- with a branch from paradise, presented by him to the MostHoly Virgin, or with a shining lantern in his right hand and with a mirror made of jasper -- in his left.

Raphael -- holds a vessel with healing medications in his left hand, and with his right hand leads Tobias, carrying the fish [for healing -- Tobit 5-8].

Uriel -- in raised right hand hold a bare sword at the level of his chest, and in his lowered left hand -- "a fiery flame".

Selaphiel -- in a prayerful posture, gazing downwards, hands folded to the chest.

Jehudiel -- in his right hand holds a golden crown, in his left -- a whip of three red (or black) branches.

Barachiel -- on his garb are a multitude of rose blossoms.

Jeremiel -- holds in his hand balance-scales.

(© 1997 by translator Fr. S. Janos, comprising pages 253-257 in Tome 2 of the Tom 2-3 "Месяцеслов" Saint-Lives Kalendar, included within the "Настольная Книга Священнослужителя" reference-book series for clergy-servers, изданние Московской Патриархии, Москва, 1978). Also *please note, that this is not material written by N. A. Berdyaev.*

frsj Publications

1.) **N. A. BERDYAEV** *"The Philosophy of Inequality"*
    1st English Translation of Berdyaev's 1918/1923 book,
    "Filosofia neravenstva" (Kl. № 20).
    (ISBN-13: 9780996399203 / ISBN-10: 0996399208)
    406 pages (6/4/15)

2.) **N. A. BERDYAEV** *"The Spiritual Crisis of the Intelligentsia"*
    1st English Translation of Berdyaev's 1910 book,
    "Dukhovnyi krizis intelligentsii" (Kl. № 4).
    (ISBN-13: 9780996399210 / ISBN-10: 0996399216)
    346 pages (6/19/15)

3.) **FR. ALEKSANDR MEN'** *"Russian Religious Philosophy: 1989-1990 Lectures"* -- 1st English Translation
    Published in 25th Year Commemoration of Fr Men' Memory
    (ISBN-13: 9780996399227 / ISBN-10: 0996399224)
    (ISBN-13: 9780996399265 / ISBN-10: 0996399267) *Paperback*
    214 pages (7/14/15)

4.) **E. SKOBTSOVA (MOTHER MARIA)**
    "The Crucible of Doubts: Khomyakov, Dostoevsky, Solov'ev, In Search of Synthesis -- Four 1929 Works".
    (ISBN-13: 9780996399234 / ISBN-10: 0996399232)
    166 pages (5/20/16) 1st English Translation

5.) **N. A. BERDYAEV** *"The Fate of Russia"*
    1st English Translation of Berdyaev's 1918 book,
    "Sud'ba Rossii". (Kl. № 15).
    (ISBN-13: 9780996399241 / ISBN-10: 0996399240)
    250 pages (10/1/16)

6.) **N. A. BERDYAEV** "*Aleksei Stepanovich Khomyakov*"
   1st English Translation of Berdyaev's 1912 book,
   "*Алексей Степанович Хомяков*" (Кl. № 6).
   (ISBN-13: 9780996399258 / ISBN-10: 0996399259)
   224 Pages (5/8/17)

7.) **N. A. BERDYAEV** "*Astride the Abyss of War and Revolutions: Articles 1914-1922*" -- 1st English Translation of a collection of 98 articles penned by Berdyaev covering the period of WWI & Russian 1917 Revolutions
   (ISBN-13: 9780996399272 / ISBN-10: 0996399275)
   (ISBN-13: 9780996399289 / ISBN-10: 0996399283) *Paperback*
   742 pages (7/24/17)

*   *   *

Forthcoming Works in Preparation:

N. A. BERDYAEV "*Sub Specie Aeternitatis: Essays Philosophic, Social and Literary (1900-1906)*".
   1st English Translation of Berdyaev's 1907 book,
   "*Sub specie aeternitatis. Опыты философские, социальные и литературные (1900-1906 гг.)*". (Кl. № 3).

N. A. BERDYAEV "*The Philosophy of Freedom*"
   1st English Translation of Berdyaev's 1911 book,
   "*Filosofiia svobody*" (Кl. № 5).

www.ingramcontent.com/pod-product-compliance
Lightning Source LLC
Chambersburg PA
CBHW070429010526
44118CB00014B/1967